PRAYING THE F
OF THE KINGI

Biblical reflections and prayer ideas

Penny Valentine

A *Praying God's Word* Resource

Eastbourne

First published 2012

ISBN 978-1-907228-17-9

Published by Tahilla Press
e-mail: tahillapress@tahilla.com

DEDICATION

This book is dedicated to the memory of
Dwight A Pryor
Teacher, mentor and friend
Who truly walked in the dust of his rabbi, Jesus

CONTENTS

FOREWORD

'Your Word, O LORD, is eternal; it stands firm in the heavens. Your faithfulness continues through all generations; You established the earth and it endures.' Psalm 118:89-90

It is usually of great interest to step back awhile and take note of how the One Who holds our lives in His hands causes our lives to intersect and to interact with those of others. I am deeply grateful for the times our faithful Lord has caused the paths of my late husband, Dwight Pryor, and I to cross with those of Rod and Penny Valentine. This interaction spans many years and various countries - Southern Africa, the United Kingdom, the United States and, at the heart of it all, Israel.

Dear reader, at this time of history we find ourselves at a critical juncture when the nations of the world are aligning themselves against this small and particular piece of land. It is the place our God chose to place His Name forever and we are enjoined to examine our hearts and to take a stand. There is only one solid place upon which to stand and that is on the Word and character of the Creator of all - the God of Abraham, Isaac and Jacob; the God of Israel.

As a key factor pertaining to this significant phase of history, Penny Valentine, in her previous books, *Praying for the Peace of Jerusalem* and *Praying for Israel and the Arab Nations,* stressed the vital necessity of prayer and intercession for Israel and the Middle East, in the light of God's Word. In this publication, she focuses on the value of the study of the Scriptures and, in particular, the demarcated weekly *parasha* (portion) of its foundation - the first five books of Moses, the Torah - as read in synagogues and studied in an annual cycle by Jewish people around the world. Apart from the edification and nurturing of the spirit this provides, it also proves to be a springboard for focussed and Scripture-oriented prayer for the extension of God's Kingdom in the nations. The same Spirit of God that inspired the Word stirs our hearts to pray in response.

In both instances, those of intercession and the study of the Torah, Penny, with her extraordinary sensitivity and dedication, touches on and reveals the heart of God, our Father, as exquisitely demonstrated in the life of Jesus.

As you partake of these studies, may your life richly intersect and interact with His Word of Truth, for the sake of His glorious Name.

Keren Hannah Pryor
Vice President, Center for Judaic Christian Studies
www.jcstudies.com

ACKNOWLEDGMENTS

I owe many of the insights in this book to others, who have stimulated and confirmed my own understanding and from whom I have learned so much. Foremost among them are our dear friends the late Dwight Pryor and his wife, Keren Hannah, of the Center for Judaic-Christian Studies in Ohio, USA. Dwight's clear thinking, deep knowledge of the Hebrew Scriptures, and above all his steadfast devotion to his master Jesus, have been a great inspiration over many years. I dedicate this book to Dwight's memory and pray that it may serve, as his own teaching does, to bring God's people closer to Himself.

Keren, herself a serious student of the Scriptures and an inspirational writer on the Torah from her perspective as a Jewish disciple of Jesus, graciously agreed to write the foreword in the midst of her many other commitments. Thank you Keren!

I thank Fiona Lindsay once again for her editing skills and unfailing encouragement and prayer for Rod and me, and Roger Stanway for painstakingly 'field testing' each study and giving helpful suggestions to improve sense and clarity. Many friends both far and near have prayed for me and this project and I deeply appreciate every one of you, believing that prayer is what will give this book power to change lives.

Finally, my husband Rod has been my primary proof reader, researcher and general encourager and always helped me focus on what was really important. As always, he deserves the most thanks of all.

Penny Valentine
December 2011

INTRODUCTION

Every builder knows that the most important part of any building is the foundation. Get that part wrong, and you're in trouble. Whatever is built upon it will be affected, and mistakes will prove dangerous and costly to put right. Jesus warned us about this in his parable about the houses built on the sand and the rock in Matthew 7:21. Only those whose foundations are strong will be able to withstand the force of the storm, and our foundations as His followers are laid through hearing and obeying His word, His teachings; the *Torat Yeshua*.

Jesus in His life on earth was a Jewish rabbi (teacher) and His teaching was based solidly on the foundation of the Hebrew Scriptures – the only Bible He had! Like Jewish people today, He knew the Old Testament as the Law, the Prophets and the Writings (*Torah*, *Neviim* and *Ketuvim* in Hebrew). The *Torah*, the first five books attributed to Moses, is itself the firm foundation on which the rest of Scripture is built. References to it are liberally sprinkled throughout the whole Bible, though many do not know the Hebrew Scriptures well enough to spot them. Certainly all the teaching of Jesus and the apostles, and thus all Christian theology, is rooted in the fundamental truths of the *Torah*, the Law of Moses. Actually 'Law' is a misleading translation; 'instruction' or 'teaching' conveys the meaning better.

The *Torah* itself is based on two great pillars of truth – Creation and Covenant. These themes are the basis of God's relationship with our world. He is sovereign over the world because He created it, and also because He has committed Himself to it in spite of the effects of sin and rebellion against His rule. He has bound Himself by unbreakable covenant to those He has redeemed from darkness and slavery to be His people. In so doing, He has inaugurated His Kingdom on earth, to challenge and defeat the powers of darkness that have usurped his authority over men and set up their own kingdoms of this world. He thereby affords all men, and ultimately the entire creation, the opportunity to be likewise redeemed.

The first two books, Genesis and Exodus, themselves lay the foundation for the other three books of the *Torah*. That is why they are so important in our understanding of the Kingdom of God. This Kingdom of God, or Kingdom of Heaven as Matthew refers to it in a typically Jewish way, forms the primary focus of Jesus' teaching. God's Kingdom is not merely to come one day in the future, although it will be consummated fully at the end of days. It is a present reality, breaking in with the power of God to restore His rule and reign in the daily lives of men.

Jesus throughout his time on earth not only taught about God's Kingdom, but demonstrated it through his blameless life and miracles of healing, even before His atoning death on the cross overcame the powers of darkness and removed Satan's legal right to rule. He did not come to found a new religion, but to further reveal and absolutely fulfill God's salvation purposes as recorded from the beginning to the end of our Bible. Right from the start, God intended to restore His loving rule and reign to the world He had created through the life, death and resurrection of His Son, the Messiah or 'Anointed One' promised beforehand to His people.

The books of Genesis and Exodus reveal God's name and character. He is lord of space and time, ruler over nature and history, and He supremely desires loving relationship with those He has created in His image. It is interesting that the earliest biblical manuscripts in English that survive today are Anglo-Saxon paraphrases of Genesis and Exodus, attributed to Caedmon in the seventh century. William Tyndale, whose passion to translate the Bible into English for the common man eventually cost him his life, considered these books only second in importance to the New Testament.

For many centuries our Western society has been based on the Judeo/Christian principles found in the Bible. Today those foundations are all but crumbled away, and we see the effects in a multitude of ways. How important it is then to strengthen what remains through persevering prayer – for ourselves, our churches and communities and the nations of the world. Thus these studies are designed to help us reflect on the foundation principles of God's Kingdom and apply them in prayer. Jesus taught his disciples in Acts 1:8 to begin their witness in Jerusalem and move outwards to the ends of the earth, and so we begin with what is closest to us, ourselves, and then move on to pray for others. We can only extend God's rule through prayer if we are prepared to accept it and submit to it in our own lives. Likewise, if we base our prayers on God's declared will as revealed clearly in His word, we know that He hears us and will answer (1 John 5:14).

All of us have people, communities and nations that God has already laid on our hearts, so I have left many prayer requests quite general, for individuals to apply as they are led by the Holy Spirit. However, some studies lend themselves to prayer for specific nations, especially the people of Israel who still play a central and vital part in God's Kingdom purposes.

As with previous books in this series, I have kept to 40 studies, although this meant leaving out many wonderful chapters. Thus they can be used for Lent study or by prayer groups as well as in personal devotions. All Scripture is from the English Standard Version unless otherwise indicated, and Hebrew words are shown in italics. I have used the word 'man' in a general sense to refer to both men and women who are equal in God's sight.

I hope that the taste of Torah that is provided here will encourage readers to delve further into the books of Moses for themselves, using some of the excellent tools available for this purpose today. A list of some I have found helpful is given at the end of this book.

May you be blessed as you study God's word, and may many others be blessed as you turn His Word into prayer for His Kingdom to come and His will to be done, on earth as it is in heaven!

Penny Valentine
pennyprayer@gmail.com

'If the foundations are destroyed, what can the righteous do?'
Psalm 11:3

'In the beginning God created the heavens and the earth' (Genesis 1:1).

 Passage for study and prayer: Genesis 1:1-2:3

In Hebrew, the book of Genesis is simply titled *'Beresheet'*, meaning 'beginnings', and on it is built all the later teachings and revelation of the Bible. The basic truth that God is, and that He created all that we know in our material universe, underpins everything. He has infinite power, because without Him, the world would not be. He is the source of form, of light, of life – of everything that is good, for indeed His creation is very good. (By the way, the word for God in Hebrew is *Elohim*. It is a plural noun, but it usually takes a singular form of the verb, implying plurality in unity – think about that one!)

The pinnacle of creation is man – made male and female, but both made in the image of God, able to reflect His nature and character in a unique way. Because of this, mankind is called to multiply and rule, under God, over His creation and have dominion over every part of it. The Kingdom of God involves the whole earth - and men, as God's stewards, are to be caretakers of it. Their relationship with the created world is a blessing given by God and is to be used for His purposes – a theme which is developed more fully in the following chapter.

It is interesting to note that although man is thus unique and superior to the rest of creation, He is not the centre of everything, as today's secular humanists would have us believe. No, this place is reserved for the Creator alone. Notice how many times the word 'God' occurs in this passage, compared to the word 'man'! Humanism by its very nature, in placing man at the centre of the universe, denies the existence of God and therefore works against His Kingdom in every possible way. No wonder absolute denial of the fact of Creation is the foundation of secular humanism in our world today. The theory of evolution is in reality a belief system based on faith, having at its core the need to justify man's existence without God. It continually has to be modified in the light of ongoing scientific discoveries, which in themselves are often consistent with the biblical account of creation.

 Pray the Word

Thank God for His creation, that wonderfully mirrors His majesty, beauty and love! **Praise** Him that as Creator, He still has absolute power to use His creation in any way He chooses to speak to people, and **pray** that many may find Him through the witness of what He has made. *'And God said, Let there be light. And there was light. And God saw the light that it was good. And God divided between the light and the darkness'* (vv3, 4).

Pray against the spirit of humanism which denies God as Creator and insists that human wisdom is superior to God's revealed truth. Especially **pray** that the doctrine of evolution will be undermined and exposed as mere theory, by recent scientific evidence that many scientists realize is inconsistent with it. **Pray** for Christians in the fields of science and education to have wisdom and influence, and that truth will prevail over deception in the minds of young people as Western educational systems teach humanism founded on the theory of evolution as a matter of course: *'Then God said, "Let the earth bring forth the living creature according to its kind...and it was so"'* (v24).

Pray that men might realize that they are created in God's image, and recognize His image in others also. **Pray** too that they may fulfil their God-given mandate to care for our world in a responsible way: *'And God created man in His image; in the image of God He created him; male and female He created them. Then God blessed them, and God said to them, "Be fruitful, and multiply and fill the earth, and subdue it; have dominion..."'* (vv27, 28).

'And the LORD God formed man of the dust of the ground, and breathed into his nostrils the breath of life; and man became a living being' (Genesis 2:7).

 Passage for study and prayer: Genesis 2:4-25

The second chapter of Genesis views the Creation and the Creator from a different perspective. Whilst in chapter one, God is only referred to as *Elohim*, here he has two names – the LORD God, or *YHWH Elohim*. YHWH is God's personal, covenant name, rendered LORD in the English Bible. Wherever it is used in Scripture, it is in the context of committed, reciprocal relationship. Whereas the first account emphasizes God's power and majesty and total 'otherness', the second stresses His love for His own creation, and especially man.

And so man is central in this second account – because God loves him. The LORD's tender love breathes through every part of this passage. God makes man (Hebrew: *'adam'*) from the dust of the earth (*'adamah'*) and breathes His breath into him to make him a living soul. He is both earthly, like the plants and animals later created for his blessing, and also totally different because he has within himself something of the divine nature. God places him in a beautiful garden providing him not only with the means of life, but of purpose and the potential for fellowship. He should not be alone, so the one that Adam calls woman, bone of his bone, is made from him, for him. The marriage relationship, joining a man and a woman in committed intimacy, and intended to mirror mankind's relationship with God, is here established for all time as the fundamental building block of human family and society.

So does this focus on man justify humanism? No, because God is still in charge. And although His love surrounds the human family, and they have all they need in Him and what He has given to them, there are boundaries too. They have one prohibition. This single command not to eat from the tree of the knowledge of good and evil was for their protection, because only God can truly judge between good and evil – but perhaps even more importantly, it was to test their own loving obedience to their Creator and their trust in Him, and to enable them to relate freely to Him with their whole being. In His wisdom the LORD gave man moral responsibility and the ability to make choices, and thus reciprocate His love.

 Pray the Word

Thank the LORD for His gift of life and love, and for His love for you, personally! **Pray** for those He brings to mind who need to know the blessing of His love. May He breathe upon them by His Holy Spirit: *'And the LORD God … breathed... the breath of life'* (v7).

Pray for those whom God has joined you to in special relationship – spouse, family, friends, colleagues, that you may be a blessing to them as God has blessed you. *'And the LORD God said, "It is not good that man should be alone; I will make him a helper comparable to him"'* (v18).

Ask God to increase your love for Him and also to give you His love for all men made in His image. **Pray** for His heart for Israel, and for all the nations and peoples of the world. *'I have found David the son of Jesse, a man after My own heart, who will do all My will'* (Acts 13:22).

Pray too that He will make you an intercessor and use you to further His purposes through your prayers. *'Ask of Me, and I shall give the nations for Your inheritance; and the uttermost parts of the earth for Your possession'* (Psalm 2:8).

'And they heard the voice of the LORD God walking in the garden in the cool of the day, and Adam and his wife hid themselves from the presence of the LORD God among the trees of the garden' (Genesis 3:8).

 Passage for study and prayer: Genesis 3:1-24

How did it all go so wrong? Adam and his wife were created to enjoy fellowship with God, yet here they were running from his presence, ashamed of their nakedness, clumsily trying to hide themselves with little bits of the garden the LORD had given them for their blessing. They had failed the test, seduced by the serpent's cunning into first questioning God's word and then disobeying it, overcome by desire to be like God, to know and judge between good and evil. They had declared their independence from their Maker and the results were cataclysmic – for mankind, for the creation, and even ultimately for God Himself.

Together with sin, fear and guilt and shame and blame enter the garden. The judgment is immediate. Though the original blueprint for man remains, to be fulfilled in family relationships and in caring for creation - it will be forever marred. Pain, fear, abuse of power, unfulfilled longings, toil, sweat and tears will mark mankind even as men continue the mandate from God to multiply and fill the earth and subdue it. The very creation becomes cursed by disobedience, and death and decay enters in. Above all, man has to be banished from the garden and the tangible, intimate presence of God, his Creator. He may no longer access the tree of life, but is made subject to death, so that evil itself will not become immortal.

Yet even here, there is a glimmer of hope. The curse upon the serpent carries the hint that one day, there could come of the seed of the woman, one who would crush the serpent's head. And God's compassion does not fail. Before He banishes them from the garden, He clothes them with skins to replace the inadequate leaf coverings they had made in their own wisdom. Animals die for their covering – a result of the Fall. Blood is shed to provide protection – foreshadowing other great coverings the LORD will provide in the future, in His gracious plan to restore His rule to the heart of man.

 Pray the Word

Thank God for His mercy and grace, that covers sinful man in so many ways. Ask forgiveness for the sin of doubting, distorting and disobeying God's Word, as Eve did. **Pray** for the church – in your nation and worldwide – to return to the Word of God as the basis for faith and practice. *'Has God indeed said, 'You shall not...?'* (v1).

Pray for families affected by sin in the nations of the world, as God leads you. **Pray** especially for women and children in cultures where they are oppressed, neglected or exploited. *'I will greatly multiply your sorrow and your conception; in pain you shall bring forth children; your desire shall be toward your husband, and he shall rule over you'* (v16).

Pray also for those struggling to eke out a living in poverty-stricken countries where godlessness is often a factor in keeping men bound in the fight to survive. Cry out to God for His mercy and salvation from the curse of sin. *'The ground is cursed for your sake. In pain shall you eat of it all the days of your life'* (v17).

'The LORD said to Cain, "Why are you angry, and why has your face fallen? If you do well, will you not be accepted? And if you do not do well, sin is crouching at the door. Its desire is for you, but you must rule over it"' (Genesis 4:6, 7).

 Passage for study and prayer: Genesis 4:1-16

Sin now becomes part of the human experience. The story of Adam's sons Cain and Abel tells us much about how it operates in our lives, and how God responds to sin in both justice and mercy – two foundational aspects of His character and Kingdom. Notice that though banished from the Garden, Adam's family still has a relationship with God. The brothers worship Him with thank offerings of the fruit of their labours, but only Abel's worship is acceptable (v4). (Some think this was because Cain's offering did not involve bloodshed, but the Hebrew word used here is *minchah,* a gift or freewill offering, not *zabach,* used to denote blood sacrifice.) The key may be that Abel gave the 'fat portions', implying in Hebrew 'the very best'.

Somehow, Cain's offering 'misses the mark' – the meaning of *chatah,* root of the word used here for sin. This in itself is not so bad – if he chooses in the future to do well, he will be accepted (v7). The real problem is that Cain's angry, sulky response opens a door for anger and envy to gain control of his life. Rather than heeding God's gracious warning to repent, and acknowledging and mastering this beast within, he chooses to let it control him more and more, until it finally bursts forth in angry words and leads to murder (v 8 – compare Jesus' words in Matthew 5:21, 22).

God's justice demands that Cain is held accountable for his crime against Abel (v10) and faces the inevitable consequences. Sin has led to death and the breaking of relationship, the very purpose of man's creation. Not only is the family broken, but Cain's relationship with the earth is now cursed too (v12). He can no longer till the soil and have anything to offer to God. Worst of all, he is banished far from the Lord's presence and protection (vv14, 16). Sin has isolated him and he fears for his own life at the hands of others.

Yet God's justice is always joined with His compassion and mercy. Man has freewill, and the LORD does his utmost to warn Cain and encourage him to choose the right path. When he does not, judgment must fall, but even in this there is grace. The brand He placed on Cain was not punishment, but protection; to keep him from man's vengeance, and to warn others of the grave consequences of harming their fellow men.

 Pray the Word

Thank God for the privilege of worshipping Him, and ask Him to convict and cleanse you of sinful heart attitudes as you enter into His presence. *'Who …shall stand in his holy place? He who has clean hands and a pure heart'* (Psalm 24:3, 4). **Pray** for sensitivity to know when sin is lying in wait for you, and grace to fight and master it.

Praise God that He sees when evil men oppress the innocent, and holds them accountable: *'The voice of your brother's blood is crying to me from the ground'* (v10). **Pray** for His intervention to bring both justice and comfort to those who are suffering unjustly because they love God or are standing firm on matters of conscience.

Pray that the social and economic problems within your own community and society may be seen for what they are, the consequences of sin: *'When you work the ground, it shall no longer yield to you its strength'* (v12). **Ask** God in His mercy to cut through false justification and deception and bring conviction and a return to the moral standards of His word. *"Where is Abel your brother?" He said, "I do not know; am I my brother's keeper?"'* (v9). Especially **pray** for the healing of broken relationships through the power of the gospel of Jesus the Messiah.

'The LORD saw that the wickedness of man was great in the earth, and that every intention of the thoughts of his heart was only evil continually. And the LORD was sorry that he had made man on the earth, and it grieved him to his heart' Genesis 6:5, 6).

 Passage for study and prayer: Genesis 6:1-7:5

After Cain's judgment, the problem of evil did not end. Although Seth was born to Adam and Eve to replace Abel and continue a more godly line, the genealogies of the next chapters show that as mankind increased on the earth, so evil did too. With one or two exceptions, even Seth's descendants lived without relating to God. Evil had taken on a deeper spiritual dimension too, with the 'sons of God', usually taken to refer to fallen angels or demonic beings, further corrupting the human race through seducing human women (vv1-4). Whoever they were, the occult strength of the resulting offspring (the *nephilim,* often translated 'giants') only magnified and increased their violent and wicked influence upon the earth in succeeding generations, in spite of God's attempt to limit this by shortening the human lifespan (v3).

This rampant wickedness infected the whole creation, including the animals (vv 7, 12), but most of all, it brought deep pain to God. The joyous delight He had felt in His good creation was replaced by such sorrow and grief that he wished he had never made man. This being had originally been created to rule over the earth as His second-in-command, and to reflect His own nature in loving relationship with Him. Yet he was now entirely evil, inside and out, in total rebellion against the LORD's good purposes for His world. It was unbearable; destruction of all living things seemed the only answer (see 6:7, 13 and 7:4).

'But Noah' (6:8). This is the first of many places in Scripture where the little word 'but' assumes huge significance. Here was one man who, like his great-grandfather Enoch (Genesis 5:24), was

22

different from those around him and had a real relationship with God (v9). Noah brought hope for the entire creation, enabling the LORD in His grace and mercy, to make a fresh start after the failure of all the other descendants from Adam. God's detailed instructions for building an ark to be a place of shelter and rescue from the coming judgment were followed by Noah to the letter. His righteous obedience won salvation for his family and for the entire natural world (vv6:22, 7:5), foreshadowing another man in another time whose greater obedience bought a greater salvation. Noah must have brought great comfort to the heart of God.

 Pray the Word

Reflect on the amazing truth that our actions and attitudes can bring both grief and joy to God's heart. **Pray** that through the power of the Holy Spirit, you may choose daily to live in obedience to His life-giving Word, for His blessing, and also your own. *'Noah did this; he did all that God commanded him'* (v22).

Give thanks that God's heart of mercy longs to save those who will listen to Him in the midst of His necessary judgment. **Pray** for those suffering as a result of flooding or other natural disasters, which are themselves often a result of man's greed, pride or sinful abuse of the environment. In their distress, may they seek and find God's salvation through Jesus. *'Everything that is on the earth shall die. But I will establish my covenant with you'* (vv17, 18).

Praise God too for the impact that those who find favour with Him can have on the world around them. **Pray** that godly men and women with His anointing will be raised up in positions of influence and authority in the nations, and **pray** for them to make decisions in line with God's Kingdom principles, that will bring healing and life to our society and our planet. *'But Noah found favour in the eyes of the LORD'* (v8).

'And when the LORD smelled the pleasing aroma, the LORD said in his heart, "I will never again curse the ground because of man, for the intention of man's heart is evil from his youth... While the earth remains, seedtime and harvest, cold and heat, summer and winter, day and night, shall not cease"' (Genesis 8:21, 22).

 Passage for study and prayer: Genesis 8:14-9:17

After the flood, there was a brand new beginning. Noah came out of the ark into a renewed, fresh world, and the first thing he did was to worship the LORD with animal sacrifices, giving God His rightful place as King over the creation. God's joyful response was to renew His blessing upon both Noah and the animals and to re-commission them all again to be fruitful and multiply. It seemed like a re-run of Genesis 1 – and yet some things were very different.

The Fall can never be undone. All mankind is born with a tendency to evil, so the ultimate answer to the problem of sin had to come from God Himself. The LORD now committed Himself to His creation in a new way. He made an unconditional covenant promise that He would never again destroy all life on earth, and He established the pattern of the seasons, the cycle of life through which He would later teach His covenant people much about His Kingdom rule. The idea of covenant, *brit,* is fundamental in Scripture. It is a legal term for a binding commitment on the part of at least one person to others, and is officially sealed with a sign, in this case, the rainbow. Rainbows form when light and water come together in the air. These are the three things needed for life, and so every rainbow is a reminder of God's faithful promise to maintain life on earth as long as earth remains.

New rules were also given for the way man related to the world. His power over the animals was greater (compare 9:2 with 1:28), and he could now use them to sustain his own life (v3) – but with an important proviso. No eating of anything while its blood was

24

still in its body, for blood is the essence of life. And life is sacred. To kill a person is to usurp God's prerogative to end life, and treats a man like an animal not made in God's image. Therefore if a man or animal sheds man's lifeblood, his life is forfeit in exchange. Though capital punishment is considered archaic and inhumane in the humanistic West, it actually expresses a very high regard for human life. Such societies undervalue life in their attitudes to abortion and even euthanasia, creating a culture of death, with ever-rising levels of violent crime.

 ## Pray the Word

Praise God for new beginnings! *The steadfast love of the LORD never ceases; his mercies never come to an end; they are new every morning; great is your faithfulness'* (Lamentations 3:22, 23). **Pray** that you may begin every day with thanksgiving for God's love, forgiveness and provision, no matter what has happened the day before!

Pray that Christians everywhere will be given a fuller understanding of the wonderful concept of covenant – God's unconditional, total commitment to those who don't deserve it. **Pray** that confidence in His utter faithfulness to His promises will undergird all who face difficulties and suffering this day. *'When the bow is in the clouds, I will see it and remember the everlasting covenant between God and every living creature of all flesh that is on the earth'* (v16).

Pray for God's mercy for nations where life is undervalued – through abortion, murder for gain, suicide bombings, honour killings, or simply marginalising the handicapped. **Pray** for those ministering to the victims of such practices. **Pray** too that the Church will both intercede and speak out about the value of human life, that the Holy Spirit may transform attitudes and practices through revelation of His Word. *'Whoever sheds the blood of man, by man shall his blood be shed, for God made man in his own image'* (vv5, 6).

'And the Lord said, "Indeed the people are one and they all have one language, and this they begin to do; now nothing that they propose to do will be withheld from them'" (Genesis 11:6).

 Passage for study and prayer: Genesis 10:1 - 11:9

Whilst previous chapters have focused on man's relationship with the Creation, Genesis 10 describes the origin of nations. Clans and tribes descended from Noah's sons Shem, Ham and Japheth spread out north, south, east and west from the Middle East after the flood, each developing their own language and settling specific territory. This gives us a general satellite view, but then we suddenly zoom in – to the valley of Shinar in modern Iraq. Here, Nimrod, the mighty leader, had a city called Babel (10:8-10); and in 11:1-9, we come really close up to find out why languages and territories were divided, and how Babel (Babylon) became the city which in Scripture always symbolises the world system –in other words, all that the Kingdom of God is not.

Without God, man's great creative gifts can so easily be used for selfish gain, for pride, for power. Here we see how man can unite for evil. The men of this first city joined together to build themselves a stronghold and tower. Perhaps they wished to bring everyone under their dominion, or simply wanted to exalt themselves above all others, or even challenge God Himself. At any rate, the tower was also designed to reach towards the heavens, implying a quest for supernatural power. They had a common purpose and a common language, giving them great strength – a very dangerous situation. Just as in the Garden, and in the generations before the flood, God had to do something to protect man from himself.

The LORD's answer is to jam their communication channels. Confusion!! The Hebrew root word *balal* means to mix, scramble together, confuse, and Babel and Babylon are names derived from this root. (So is *balagan* – the very descriptive Hebrew word that today can be applied to everything from congested city traffic to a teenager's bedroom!) The result is exactly what the people of Babel didn't want. Their building was never completed, and with lack of communication came disunity and separation. Men went their separate ways, which of course in this case was God's original plan, for them to fill the earth and subdue it (Genesis 1:28; 9:1). Notice that His purpose for mankind was fulfilled even through His judgment.

 Pray the Word

Thank God once again that even his judgments are a result of his mercy. **Ask** Him to deliver you from the sins of selfishness, pride and a desire to control others and help you to use your God-given gifts for His glory alone. *'Create in me a clean heart, O God, and renew a right spirit within me'* (Psalm 51:10). **Pray** the same for His people Israel, and for the Church worldwide.

Pray earnestly that the Lord will bring confusion to all the efforts of the world system to hinder the growth of the Kingdom of God. As you follow current world news, ask for insight and **pray** that He will confuse those who are uniting for evil against His Kingdom and His people, including both Israel and the church. *'Your Kingdom come, your will be done…'* (Luke 11:2).

Pray for the great cities of the world, so filled with sin, poverty and suffering but also with many opportunities for God's grace to enter at the point of man's need. **Pray** for those offering His love and hope to city-dwellers everywhere, and ask God to raise up powerful expressions of His Kingdom in the midst of darkness and confusion. *'Where sin abounded, grace abounded much more…'* (Romans 5:20).

'Now the LORD had said to Abram: "Get out of your country, from your family and from your father's house, to a land that I will show you. I will make you a great nation; I will bless you and make your name great; and you will be a blessing."' (Genesis 12:1, 2)

 Passage for study and prayer: Genesis 12:1-9

Up until now, the Genesis account has dealt in broad strokes with the momentous themes of creation, the problem of sin and evil and the division of men into different nations and peoples. Now, there is a sudden change of focus. Once again the zoom lens brings us up close – to see the beginning of God's answer to Adam's sin, the first step in the restoration of His rule to the heart of man. The LORD acts, quite simply, to call one man into a particular spot on the earth and into a special relationship with Him. Abram, a descendant of Shem, is told to leave his country, his relatives, all his security, and go to a land which the LORD will show him. The purpose is clear: he is to be the start of a new nation, a great nation – one that will be blessed to be a blessing. It will all happen through his getting to know the LORD.

This call is to Abram personally, but it extends to his descendants too (v7). Just as the nations are separated into their specific territories, so this new nation is to live in a specific place, because here, God's redemptive purposes are to be played out. This particular and special land will be the focus of what God plans to do. His plan is to bless not only Abram and his family, but through them, all the families of the earth. The gospel is for the nations! (Paul agrees - see Galatians 3:8.)

What's more, this people will not only be the vehicle of revelation of the true God, they will also be a standard by which all other nations and peoples will be judged by Him. Verse 3 is quite clear – those who bless them will be blessed, and those who curse them will be cursed. Why? Because they represent God Himself amongst the nations, and they still have that calling today.

Abram obeyed (unlike Adam!) and went (v4), and as a result his relationship with God and knowledge of Him grew (vv7, 8). As he wandered through the land, he built altars of sacrifice and worship, physical places to seek the LORD, testimony to the true God beginning to be established in the land God had chosen for His Kingdom purposes.

 Pray the Word

Praise the Lord for His mighty plan of salvation, which all began with the obedience of one man! **Pray** that you too may clearly hear and obey God's voice, so that you may know Him more and more, and be used as He chooses in His Kingdom. *'So Abram departed as the LORD had spoken to him...'* (v4).

Pray for your church and nation to be blessed with a deeper knowledge of God, through being a blessing to God's people Israel. *'And I will bless those that bless you and curse the one who curses you'* (v3). **Stand** against the spirit of anti-Semitism that causes people to despise or revile Israel and the Jewish people, even within the church, and pray for a revelation of the truth of this promise.

Give thanks, as you think of the Bible, and our Redeemer Jesus who died for the whole world, that God's promise to Abram has been fulfilled: *'in you shall all families of the earth be blessed'* (v3). **Thank** God too that modern Israel has blessed the world in many ways during its short history as a nation, and **pray** that He will continue to use Israeli doctors, scientists and agriculturalists to pioneer new breakthroughs for the benefit of mankind.

'On the same day the LORD made a covenant with Abram, saying, "I have given this land to your seed, from the river of Egypt to the great river, the river Euphrates..."' (Genesis 15:18, NKJV)

 Passage for study and prayer: Genesis 15:1-21

What else happened on this 'same day'? Surely Abram never forgot it. One wonders if he was despairing of God's promises – although he had experienced victory and blessing in the land, yet after ten long years there was no sign of a son, let alone many descendants. He had many questions in his heart, and God knew it. He came to Abram in a very personal way, and spoke to him: "I" - and the Hebrew is extremely emphatic here – "am your shield (protection) and your exceedingly great reward" (v1). The real focus of all God's promises is Himself; all His blessings come from who He is. He is love, and He is omnipotent – He can do the impossible, and He is all we need.

Thus the Lord reiterates his promise (v4) that Abram will indeed have offspring from his own body, this time as numerous as the stars in the night sky, and that the land of Canaan is his inheritance (v7). These two elements, descendants and land, form the basis of the covenant the Lord was about to make with Abram, to confirm to him that He means what He says (v8). As instructed, Abram makes preparations for the ritual of 'cutting a covenant' between two parties, as generally practised at that time. Each would walk between the halves of the divided animals in a figure of eight pattern, to ratify a legally binding agreement. Having watched over the carcasses and driven off the predators, he falls into a deep sleep, in which a 'horror of great darkness' falls upon him (vv9-12). Through this awesome experience, God shows him the future of his descendants as a people in the land, before passing between the pieces as a flaming torch, thus sealing the covenant (vv13-18).

Have you noticed something here? Abram did not take part in the ritual. The commitment was all on God's part. This was an unconditional covenant, with no obligations whatever on Abram's side, and his only part was to respond in faith to God's Word and thus receive the blessings of relationship with Him. Verse 6 makes clear that Abram chose to believe God, and his faith became righteousness in God's sight. This, the first of the LORD's great covenants with the Jewish people, is based purely on faith. For this reason, it is also the foundation of the last great covenant, the new covenant of faith in the sacrifice of the Jewish Messiah, that enables all who believe to enter the Kingdom of God. What grace God shows – not only to Israel, but to those who are Abraham's descendants through faith too!

 Pray the Word

Give thanks that through God's covenant with Abram, you too by faith can know how much He is committed to you. Meditate on the LORD's promise; *'Do not be afraid... I am your shield, your exceedingly great reward'* (v1). **Pray** that you may know Him more and more as the all-sufficient one in every circumstance of your life.

Pray for all Abram's natural descendants, both Jews and Arabs, to believe God's promises, even as Abram did, and so release His blessings upon themselves. *'And he believed in the LORD, and He accounted it to him for righteousness'* (v6).

Pray that the truths of this passage, showing God's everlasting covenant and commitment to His covenant people Israel, might be known and understood by the church worldwide. *'I am the LORD, who brought you out of Ur of the Chaldeans, to give you this land to inherit it'* (v7).

'Then God said: "No, Sarah your wife shall bear you a son, and you shall call his name Isaac; I will establish My covenant with him for an everlasting covenant, and with his descendants after him"'
(Genesis 17:19, NKJV).

 Passage for study and prayer: Genesis 17:1-20

Once again, the next key moment in Abram's life begins with a special revelation from God. This time the Lord announces Himself as *El Shaddai* – Almighty God – a reminder to Abram of his awesome power and omnipotence. God can do anything – just look at v17! Notice that whereas the encounter of Chapter 15 initiated the Abrahamic covenant in an unconditional way, and was focused on the promise of the land, here the emphasis is on the other part of God's promise, the descendants (v2). The purpose of a special land is to nurture and set apart a special people who will be sealed into covenant relationship with God.

Relationship requires response. These covenant people, like their father, will be called to walk before the LORD (in His light) and be blameless, i.e. filled with integrity (v1, compare Deuteronomy 18:13). They will be set apart, just as Abram and Sarai are given new names to signify their new identity as parents of a covenant people. Abram, meaning 'exalted father', becomes Abraham, 'the father of a multitude', and his wife becomes Sarah, 'princess'. They will be set apart for relationship with their God through an everlasting covenant (v7), just as the land is an everlasting possession (v8). They will carry the sign of this covenant and the seal of their commitment to it in their very flesh, from their earliest days (vv11, 12). By this cutting act of circumcision, every male descendant of Abraham will become part of the 'set apart' people of God.

Having said all this, God then drops the bombshell. He is going to bless elderly Sarah, who has been barren for many decades, with motherhood – what a joke! Along with her name change will come a son, Isaac, meaning 'laughter', and she too will be a mother of nations. Although God loves Ishmael just as Abraham does, and will prosper and bless him, His covenant will be with Isaac, the one of His choice, the one born as a result of His promise – and His power. Election is a mystery, and some say it is unfair, but God can do what He likes, and He has His reasons. By the way, four times in this passage this covenant is described as 'everlasting' – (vv7, 8, 13, 19). Do you think God means what He says?

 Pray the Word

Meditate on the Lord's words to Abraham: *'I am God Almighty; walk before me and be blameless'* (v1). **Ask** the Lord to show you where you fall short and praise Him for His power to fulfil His perfect plan for your life. *'I will make you exceedingly fruitful'* (v6).

Give thanks that after millennia, the Jewish people today are still set apart as a corporate testimony to the faithfulness of God and the truth of His word. **Pray** for the many for whom their 'chosenness' is a burden they would rather be without. May they find the joy of knowing their God and being known by Him: *'And I will establish my covenant between me and you and your offspring after you throughout their generations for an everlasting covenant, to be God to you and to your offspring after you'* (v7).

Pray again for God's outpoured blessing on the descendants of Ishmael according to His promise, and especially that they might find spiritual life through faith in the Messiah. *'Oh that Ishmael might live before You'* (v18).

33

'I have known him, in order that he may command his children and his household after him, that they keep the way of the LORD, to do righteousness and justice and judgment, that the Lord may bring to Abraham what He has spoken to him.' (Genesis 18:19 NKJV)

 Passage for study and prayer: Genesis 18:16-33

Here we see the beginnings of the fruit of Abraham's relationship with God. God has known Abraham, so that Abraham may know Him, and teach others who He is. (Note that in Hebrew the word 'know' – *yada* – as well as the usual straightforward meanings, can also mean the intimacy of sexual union that brings forth life. It is also used for example in Genesis 4:1). Abraham is to lead his family into the life-giving ways of the LORD. He is to live by God's values of righteousness and justice and judgment, so that he may receive the promised blessings for himself and also for all the nations of the earth (v18).

To understand the impact of this, we have to see it in its context. The cities of Sodom and Gomorrah were awash with evil, and once again, God cannot let such sin continue without judgment. But now for the first time he has a man who knows something of His nature, who understands righteousness, justice and judgment because he is getting to know God. He is able to share with him what He is about to do, and why. Abraham's response to this news is profoundly touching, and the very first instance of intercession in the Bible.

As the men move off towards Sodom, Abraham approaches the LORD and reminds Him of His character. "Will not the judge of all the earth do right?" He raises the issue, still so relevant today, of the righteous being caught up in the judgment of the wicked. Surely God who is righteous and just, will not destroy the city for the lack of a few righteous? The Lord's response to Abraham's increasingly

34

daring prayer reveals His mercy, and His delight in Abraham's grasp of His character. Even though chapter 19 shows that in fact there were not even 10 righteous men in Sodom and judgment could not be avoided, surely Abraham's intercession (literally meaning 'standing between' God and men) was a factor in the almost forcible saving of his nephew Lot, and those others of his family who were willing to listen and flee.

 Pray the Word

Seek God for His insight and anointing to pray according to His purposes for the nations as you see what is happening in the world today. *'And the LORD said, "Shall I hide from Abraham what I am doing?"'* (Genesis 18:17)

Give thanks that you can 'stand between' the Lord and members of your family, and pray for His mercy over the circumstances of their lives. *'And it came to pass, when God destroyed the cities of the plain, that God remembered Abraham, and sent Lot out of the midst of the overthrow...'* (Genesis 19:29). **Pray** too to follow Abraham's example in praying for those who are suffering through the sin of others. **Pray** for those who are victims of gross sexual sin and abuse, especially in places where there is no protection for the weak or vulnerable.

Plead with God to raise up a righteous remnant in the nations who will stand in the gap for their countries. **Give thanks** for the growth of the church in the third world, where Christians are having a real impact on their society through their prayers and actions, and **pray** that this will increase even where there is persecution. *'So the LORD said, "If I find in Sodom fifty righteous within the city, then I will spare all the place for their sakes"'* (Genesis 18:26).

'And Abraham went and took the ram and offered it up as a burnt offering instead of his son. So Abraham called the name of that place, "The LORD will provide"; as it is said to this day, "On the mount of the LORD it shall be provided"'
(Genesis 22:13b, 14).

 Passage for study and prayer: Genesis 22:1-18

The Kingdom walk is a walk of faith and dependence on God's character, and Abraham illustrates it perfectly, as New Testament writers testify – check out Hebrews 11:1, 17-19 and James 2:21-23. Here, God deliberately tested Abraham (v1), to see whether firstly, he would recognize His voice, and secondly, if he would obey His word, even if it didn't seem to make sense and cost him his dearest and best (v12). Remember that Isaac embodied all the LORD's covenant promises to Abraham regarding the future. In offering up his only beloved son, Abraham was laying everything on the altar, except his covenant relationship with the LORD. He surrendered it all – trusting only that God knew what He was doing. Somehow He would work things out to fulfil His promised purpose. He told his servants that he and Isaac were going to 'worship' (v5), and would return. This Hebrew word for worship, *shachach*, literally means to bow down, or submit, and that is what this sacrifice was all about.

As James stresses in his letter, biblical faith is not mere mental assent to theological concepts and doctrines, but practical obedience to God's will, submitting to His rule over our lives, holding nothing back. Faith often requires both time and effort, and can be very hard work! Abraham had to make preparations, (I wonder what he said to Sarah?), then travel for several days, and climb up Mount Moriah with the unsuspecting Isaac. Right up to the last moments as he built the altar, tied up his son, and finally raised the knife to kill him, he was continually exercising faith in God's love, righteousness and faithfulness to make sense of it all.

36

He could only do this because of his unwavering focus on the character of God. He **knew** *Yahweh yireh,* 'the LORD will provide'. The word translated 'provide' in verses 8 and 14 is *ra'ah,* meaning to see – 'the LORD will see to it'. He knew God saw into his heart. *Ra'ah* is also used in v4, and in v13, when Abraham lifted up his eyes and saw the ram. At that moment, faith became sight. God did provide a ram for sacrifice in Isaac's place, foreshadowing future sacrifices on Mount Moriah after the Temple was built there, and ultimately the greatest sacrifice of all, His own beloved Son. Abraham's faith-filled and loving obedience finally sealed and secured God's covenant blessing for all generations to come (vv16, 17). Imagine the depth of his worship to the LORD as he and Isaac sacrificed that ram!

 Pray the Word

Praise God that faith is not based on our feelings, but on God's faithfulness. **Pray** that He will increase your faith as you seek to walk daily in worship to Him, submitting to His will. *'By myself I have sworn, declares the LORD, because you have done this and have not withheld… I will surely bless you'* (vv16, 17). **Pray** the same for others whom you know, that they may experience His outpoured blessing on their lives.

Pray for an increase of active faith in the church worldwide, based on Holy Spirit revelation of the character of God and obedience to His Word, which will issue in true worship and a release of His Kingdom power to transform situations and societies. *'You see that faith was active along with his works, and faith was completed by his works'* (James 2:22).

Pray too that Christians may know a release of God's provision in all circumstances to do His will. The great missionary Hudson Taylor said, "God's work done in God's way will never lack God's supplies". *'God will provide for himself the lamb for a burnt offering'* (v8). **Pray** that experiencing His miraculous provision may lead to the rapid extension of His Kingdom in the nations in the coming days.

'Then Isaac brought her into the tent of Sarah his mother and took Rebekah, and she became his wife, and he loved her. So Isaac was comforted after his mother's death' (Genesis 24:67).

 Passage for study and prayer: Genesis 24:1-67

Sarah's death no doubt increased Abraham's determination to find the right wife for Isaac, to secure the next generation. He knew how important it was that Isaac, the chosen son, should have a wife also chosen by the Lord – one who would not lead him astray from God's ways but be a godly influence on her children. Canaanite girls were certainly not suitable! Hence he instructed his most senior and trusted servant to travel to his own family, far away to the north-east, to seek a bride for Isaac under the guidance and direction of the LORD. Notice that she had to return with him – it was essential that Isaac should remain within the land of his inheritance, and establish the next covenant generation there (vv1-9).

The wonderful account of the servant's successful mission (vv 10-61) illustrates so much about the power of prayer, about the loving purposes of God, and about how He arranges circumstances to bring about His will. It reminds us that the marriage covenant is central to God's purposes, and that He appoints the perfect partner when the choice is submitted to Him. Rebekah was young, beautiful and willing to take this sudden, unexpected risk and obey the obvious will of God, leaving her home and family to cleave to a distant someone she hadn't even met. Isaac, on the other hand, had to trust God to make the choice for him, and be patient through what was probably many long months of waiting!

At last the moment came when he was out in the fields at the end of the day, thinking about it all, and saw the caravan approaching (v63). He went to meet it. Rachel was veiled, but having heard the story, Isaac could not doubt that she was 'the one'. When he married her, and saw beneath the veils, I'm sure he approved of God's choice! He loved her (v67). This is the second time this word for love, *ahav,* occurs in the Bible (the first is in Genesis 22:2). It belongs in a family context, and has at its root the idea of giving. Love is a gift that we both give and receive, and it is a privilege and responsibility. Strong family relationships are at the heart of God's Kingdom – no wonder marriage and the family are under such enormous attack today.

 Pray the Word

Praise God for those He has given you to love and be loved by in your own family, and **pray** for grace and strength to love and give as He loves us. *'We love because he first loved us'* (1 John 4:19).

Give thanks that marriage is fundamental to God's Kingdom and that He calls couples together to be a blessing to Him, to each other and to those around them. **Pray** that young people you know will seek God's choice of partner, and be patient to wait for His best and willing to obey His will. *'Blessed be the LORD, the God of my master Abraham, who has not forsaken his steadfast love and his faithfulness… As for me, the LORD has led me in the way'* (v27).

Pray for an increase in strong, healthy and godly marriages and families in your nation and in the nations of the world. *'Therefore a man shall leave his father and his mother and hold fast to his wife'* (Genesis 2:24). **Pray** especially for protection for Christian families, that they may be an inspiration to others and a witness of God's love and faithfulness.

Claim this promise for all in God's Kingdom: *'Blessed is everyone who fears the LORD, who walks in his ways! You shall eat the fruit of the labour of your hands; you shall be blessed, and it shall be well with you. Your wife will be like a fruitful vine within your house; your children will be like olive shoots around your table'* (Psalm 128:1-3). **Pray** too for those involved in counselling engaged or married couples.

GOD'S CHOICE, MAN'S CHOICE

'And the LORD said to her, "Two nations are in your womb, and two peoples shall be separated from your body; one people shall be stronger than the other, and the older shall serve the younger"' (Genesis 25:23).

 Passage for study and prayer: Genesis 25:11-34

This passage focuses on two sets of brothers descended from Abraham, each pair having one set aside for God's special purpose. Though Ishmael received God's promise of twelve mighty sons who founded the Arab tribes of the Near East, Isaac was heir to the covenant. And yet in spite of God's special blessing (v11), Isaac's wife was barren like his mother Sarah. It was only through his prolonged prayer over twenty years that Rebekah eventually conceived, so no wonder she was anxious when she felt her twins struggling within her. What was wrong with her long awaited pregnancy? Why were things so difficult when she thought she was being blessed by God?

The Lord's answer was startling, (and also helps to explain Rebekah's later behaviour in Chapter 27). He doesn't tell her she has two babies in her womb, but two nations. Even though they shared the same mother and father in the perfect plan of God, one of these brothers was not destined to be part of the covenant people. Why did God do this? Why not give just one son to carry the line to the third generation? Or make Jacob the natural first-born, if he was more suited to be heir to Abraham's promises? Jewish and Christian commentators suggest many answers, but we can let the Bible interpret itself. Paul points out in Romans 9:11-13 that God's choice of Jacob was before they had done anything, good or bad. Election is a mystery, a sovereign choice of the Almighty, as Malachi 1:2-3 states clearly. In fact, He usually chooses the one who has no natural advantage or priority – think of Abel and Isaac. That is good news for most of us!

However, He also allows man choice, and works through imperfect individuals. Both Jacob and Esau had character faults, as is obvious in later chapters; but their choices affected their destiny. Esau chose to satisfy the desire of a moment, and in so doing, despised his birthright, (v34) and lost his blessing. (See Genesis 27:38, Hebrews 12:16, 17). He became Edom (v30), meaning 'red' like the stew he craved; and though the people of Edom or in Greek, Idumea, lived in the southern deserts of today's Jordan and Israel for centuries, they continued to demonstrate the weaknesses of their forefather Esau until the Romans finally obliterated their national identity. King Herod, persecutor of the infant Jesus, was one of the last of the Idumeans.

Jacob, on the other hand, actively chose to pursue the blessing, and in so doing, he fulfilled God's plan for his life. He never accepted second best – his name means 'one who grasps the heel'. He was a grasper, grabbing every opportunity to get ahead. Though it often got him into trouble, and he had to learn many hard lessons on the way, he kept on pursuing his destiny. Today, the Lord still looks for those who will do likewise in His Kingdom, who will not settle for less than His best for their lives. Is He facing you with choices that will affect your destiny?

 Pray the Word

Ask Him to help you choose that which will lead to blessing and fulfilment of His perfect will for your life, and never to settle for second best. *'I have set before you life and death, blessing and cursing; therefore, choose life...so that you may love the LORD your God, that you may obey His voice, and that you may cling to Him, for He is your life'* (Deuteronomy 30:19, 20). **Pray** the same for others you know and for Christians everywhere.

Pray the same Scripture for Jacob's descendants who have returned from many nations to the Land of Israel in our day. Also **pray** it for the nomadic Bedouin people currently inhabiting the deserts of the Arava in Israel and Jordan. Followers of Islam, may they make the choices that will lead them to fullness of life in Messiah Jesus.

'Behold, I am with you, and will keep you wherever you go, and will bring you back to this land; for I will not leave you until I have done what I have spoken to you' (Genesis 28:15).

 Passage for study and prayer: Genesis 28:10-22

Jacob had tricked his father into giving him his blessing, and received a lot of trouble with it! Esau was plotting to kill him and thanks to his mother's intervention, Isaac was sending him away to find a wife among the in-laws in Syria. So no sooner had Jacob been confirmed as heir to God's promises to Abraham (see Genesis 27:28,29 and also 28:4), than he was having to leave the land that was his inheritance. I wonder if he wondered if it was worth it, as he fled for his life and left behind his family and all he knew. Jacob was the first of a countless throng of Hebrew exiles who have had to pack up and leave their homes down the ages, because of God's special calling as His covenant people.

Verse 11 tells us that Jacob came to 'a certain place' at sunset, where he lay down and slept. He used a stone for his pillow – God's doorstep! This place became his entrance to a new dimension, as he dreamed and saw the connection between earth and heaven – between the creation, where he lived, and the unknown sphere where God existed and ruled. The constant traffic of angels, God's messengers, on this heavenly escalator showed there was an intimate if usually unseen contact between the two realms. Way up at the top of the staircase was the LORD. He spoke to Jacob, affirming to him the same covenant promises about descendants, land and blessing given to his fathers. But this time, He added something – a promise of His presence. Wherever Jacob was, the LORD would be; protecting him and overruling his circumstances to bring him back to the land and fulfil His purposes for Jacob's life.

Jacob was overwhelmed as he realised he had been at the very front door of *Beit El*, God's House. He knew he had to respond, and vowed to take Yahweh as his God and honour Him, if His word proved true. He turned his pillow into a pillar, anointed with oil, to mark the spot and to stand as a testimony to God's promise that he would one day return to the land of his inheritance. (For the sequel to this story, check out Genesis 35!)

 Pray the Word

Praise God that the Kingdom of heaven is never far away when we are in relationship with Him. **Pray** that He may give you revelation of His presence with you, especially at times of difficulty or pain. *'It is the LORD who goes before you. He will be with you; he will not leave you or forsake you. Do not fear or be dismayed'* (Deuteronomy 31:8).

Pray for Jacob's descendants today who are still in exile outside the land of Israel, including many born in Israel who have moved away because of the difficulties of life there. Ask the Lord to remove every obstacle to their return and to bring them back as He has promised: *'Though I scattered them among the nations, yet in far countries they shall remember me, and with their children they shall live and return'* (Zechariah 10:9).

Pray for refugees across the world who have fled from their homes because of conflict or the collapse of their livelihoods. **Pray** that their difficult circumstances may cause them to seek and find a relationship with the true God, and **pray** that those who seek to reach them in His name may be effective channels of His love and truth. *'Where shall I go from Your Spirit? Or where shall I flee from your presence?'* (Psalm 139:7)

'And He said, "Your name shall no longer be called Jacob, but Israel; for you have struggled with God and with men, and have prevailed' (Genesis 32:28, NKJV).

 Passage for study and prayer: Genesis 32:9-32

Jacob's next direct encounter with God is very different from the last. It is many years later – he has experienced God's blessing and is returning to the land at His command as a rich man with a large family; two wives, two concubines and twelve sons, and at least one daughter! However, in returning, he has to face head-on his lurking fear of his brother Esau, who once wanted to kill him. The news of Esau's coming to meet him with 400 men, strikes terror into Jacob's heart. He does all he can think of to appease Esau and protect his family, and he prays and reminds God of his promise of protection, too (v12). But in the end, he is left alone, the only member of his huge company still on the other side of the brook, in the darkest hours of the night.

It is then that a mysterious Man appears and wrestles with Jacob. Was he trying to force him across the brook? Did Jacob's desperate fight begin as an attempt to evade doing what he dreaded? It is clear from verses 27-30 that Jacob eventually recognised this man to be God Himself - many Christians would say, a pre-incarnate appearance of Jesus. How often God's people have had to desperately wrestle with Him in order to come to a place of obedience in the face of fear! The fact is that God is more powerful than we are. When we try to fight Him we always come off worst, and Jacob's hip was dislocated. However, his helplessness makes him determined not to let go of his adversary, who in his extremity is his only hope and support. He clings close in desperation and demands a blessing!

Blessing is given – and includes a new name: Israel. From the root *sarah,* meaning to have power or to prevail, together with *el,*

44

meaning God, the meaning of Israel is often given as 'you have struggled or prevailed with God' (v28). However, according to Jewish scholars, it could simply mean 'God rules'. Jacob had finally learned to submit fully to God. His struggle had brought him into a much deeper relationship with the LORD. He called the place *Peniel,* meaning 'Face of God', because of this face to face encounter. It is significant that as the day dawned, he crosses the brook to face his brother – willingly, but with a limp that was never to leave him. From this time he was both weaker and stronger – a prince with God who had prevailed.

 Pray the Word

Praise God that in the darkest hours we can experience a 'close encounter' with Jesus that will change our lives! Ask the Lord to help you see Him, submit to Him and become the person He wants you to be. *'And Jacob called the name of the place Face of God [Peniel]; for I have seen God face to face, and my life is preserved'* (v30, NKJV).

Pray for the 'children of Israel' today as they face many fears in their difficult relationship with their brother 'Esau' – the Arabs. May they seek the face of God to help them, and may He give them wisdom and grace to enable reconciliation: *'Please deliver me from the hand of my brother, from the hand of Esau, for I fear him, that he may come and attack me, the mothers with the children'* (v11).

Pray for believers worldwide who struggle in the face of danger and severe persecution as a result of keeping faith with the Lord. **Pray** they may have faith and strength to wrestle with God in their difficult circumstances and win through to new places of intimacy with Him and victory for His Kingdom. *'But Jacob said, "I will not let you go unless you bless me'* (v26).

'This is the history of Jacob. Joseph, being seventeen years old, was feeding the flock with his brothers' (Genesis 37:2a).

 Passage for study and prayer: Genesis 37:1-36

What a strange verse this is. Look at Genesis 35:23-26, where Jacob's twelve sons are conveniently listed, and we find that Joseph was the second to youngest. Yet Jacob's story continues not with Reuben his first born, nor even with Judah, the direct ancestor of Jesus, but with Joseph. Why? Admittedly he was his father's favourite - most loved because he was the son of Jacob's old age (v3) and also no doubt because his mother was Rachel, Jacob's beloved and formerly barren wife, who had since died. But this isn't why Joseph takes centre stage. Just as with Abraham, Isaac and Jacob, the LORD has a special purpose in His Kingdom plan for this particular lad. So He begins by giving him two prophetic dreams, when he was still only a teenager, in which he is clearly elevated above the rest of the family (vv5-10).

These dreams have an unfortunate result - at least Joseph no doubt thought so at the time! Jacob's favouritism had predictably caused family strife, and it's clear that young Joseph and his older brothers didn't get on together (vv 2, 4, 5, 8). It's no wonder they did not appreciate hearing that in his dreams, they bowed down to him! Even his father rebuked him for arrogance, though he took the dreams seriously (v11). So later, when the opportunity arose in the desert, the brothers in their hatred and jealousy plotted to get rid of Joseph, and were only restrained from outright murder by Reuben and Judah. Instead, they sold him to the Ishmaelites, and deceived their father into thinking he'd been killed by wild animals. Jacob was devastated - and as for Joseph, he went from being a spoiled favourite son to a despised and captive slave, in just one day! Perhaps he found it hard to believe that his dreams had been from God.

Isn't it amazing that God uses deeply flawed human beings guilty of all manner of sinful behaviour to accomplish His sovereign purposes? Or that evil and suffering can be part of His plan? No one realised at the time that these events were setting the stage for the opening act of God's great plan of redemption – not only of His chosen people, the children of Israel, but of all mankind. Read on for the rest of the story!

Pray the Word

Praise the Lord for the special purpose that He has for you! Ask Him to make His vision your vision, and fulfil His plan for your life through every circumstance, both easy and hard, as you seek Him. *'For I know the thoughts that I think towards you, says the LORD; thoughts of peace and not of evil, to give you a future and a hope… you will seek me and find me, when you search for me with all your heart'* (Jeremiah 29:11,13).

Pray fervently for young people in your family, your community, and your nation, to receive vision from God that will direct them into His purposes for them. *'He said to them, "Hear this dream that I have dreamed…"'* (v6). **Pray** for mentors to support and guide them, and for protection from the forces of darkness that seek to steal, kill and destroy the coming generation to keep them from serving the King.

Pray for families like Joseph's, with difficult 'half' or 'step' relationships, and ask the Lord to heal those who struggle with insecurity, jealousy and hate. **Pray** for wisdom for parents in dealing with their children, and that families may find new life and hope in Jesus. *'And when his brethren saw that their father loved him more than all his brethren, they hated him, and could not speak peaceably unto him'* (v4).

'And after a time his master's wife cast her eyes on Joseph and said, "Lie with me." But he refused, and said to [her], "Behold, because of me my master has no concern about anything in the house, and he has put everything that he has in my charge ... How then can I do this great wickedness and sin against God?"' (Genesis 39:7- 9)

 Passage for study and prayer: Genesis 39:1-23

God's Kingdom people stand out from the crowd! Egypt was the most powerful, civilized nation in the ancient world, and Joseph was only a Hebrew slave brought up in the desert – yet from the start his life had an enormous impact on those around him. He knew the true God and lived under God's rule, even in an alien culture, and this made his life different. He had integrity and inner freedom, and others could see it. Moreover, by choosing to live this way, he was able to walk in God's purpose for his life. This season was a time of training and testing to prepare him for the future leadership foreshadowed by those dreams in faraway Canaan.

He could have ended up anywhere, but God put Joseph in the household of a rich and powerful official at the heart of Pharoah's court. Here, he learned both farming and business skills as he rose to become the manager over all Potiphar's affairs. His master left every decision to him, except what to have for dinner! This shows Joseph wasn't only a gifted administrator, but a trusted and hardworking man who was a wonderful witness to the Hebrew God. Clearly the LORD's presence and blessing in his life flowed through him to others and brought him great success in his sphere of influence.

However light shows up the darkness, and as so often happens, his faith in God and moral integrity also led to persecution, lies and betrayal. Potiphar's wife had her lustful eye on the handsome Hebrew slave and was infuriated and offended by his persistent refusal of her advances. When one day he literally fled from temptation, she seized her opportunity to gain revenge by unjustly accusing him of attempted rape. What a shock for Joseph! Imagine how he felt – his master thought he had betrayed his trust, his reputation was destroyed and all his satisfying work ended as he was cast into prison. However, in God's sovereign plan, this turns out to be merely the next phase of his education. His character and abilities cannot be ignored and again win him favour with the authorities. He is tasked with serving some important prisoners –all courtiers locked up on Pharoah's personal orders. Just think how much Joseph must have learned about Egyptian politics and government just by being around these men!

 Pray the Word

Meditate on Joseph's situation – are there any parallels with your own? **Pray** that you may resist temptation and be a good witness to the Lord in all circumstances. Ask Him to train you to become His faithful servant. *'So Joseph found grace in his sight, and served him.' 'How then can I do this great wickedness, and sin against God?'* (vv4, 9)

Give thanks for Joseph's example of moral integrity that never left him, despite all manner of temptations, and pray that Christians today may not be conformed to the standards of those around them, but may live holy (set apart) lives as an example to others. *'And do not be conformed to this world, but be transformed by the renewing of your mind, that you may prove what is that good and acceptable and perfect will of God'* (Romans 12:2, NKJV).

Pray for those unjustly accused and imprisoned for their faith in the nations of the world, especially in Egypt and other Muslim countries. May the LORD sustain them and turn their captivity into blessing for God's Kingdom. *'But the LORD was with Joseph and showed him steadfast love and gave him favour in the sight of the keeper of the prison'* (v21). **Pray** too for ministries reaching out to those in prison in the nations.

JOSEPH THE SAVIOUR

'And Pharaoh said to his servants, "Can we find a man like this, in whom is the spirit of God?"'
(Genesis 41:38)

 Passage for study and prayer: Genesis 41:37-57

Isn't it amazing how suddenly circumstances can change when God is in control? Divine revelation enabled Joseph to interpret the dreams of others, and led to the dramatic change from imprisoned Hebrew slave to the most honoured and powerful man in the country, in just one day! (See chapters 40 and 41.) Thirteen long years of trial and training had finally ended in an astonishing recognition of Joseph's special gifts and wisdom, all given him by the indwelling Spirit of God.

Joseph was 30 years old when Pharoah made him Governor or ruler over all Egypt. He was given fine Egyptian clothing, an Egyptian wife and an Egyptian name - the meaning is not known for sure, but some think it translates as 'the man of the bread of life', others, 'God speaks and He lives'. However despite all outward appearances, he kept his Hebrew identity and his two sons were given Hebrew names. Manasseh means 'causing to forget', and with his birth, Joseph could forget his past suffering and his lack of family. He didn't forget his God though – when Ephraim, meaning 'twice fruitful' was born, he gave God the glory for the fruitfulness of his life in exile. He also continued to live his life in the presence and power of God and so became quite literally the saviour not only of the Egyptian people, but of the entire region. As the forecast famine took hold, the only place where food was to be found was Egypt, and the only one through whom it could be obtained was Joseph himself. What a man!

Has there been another like him since? It is easy for Christians to see many parallels between the lives of Joseph and Jesus – look for them in this passage and throughout Joseph's story. Amazingly, Jewish rabbinic tradition also refers to a Messiah (literally 'anointed one') to come from God, called *'Moshiach ben Yosef'* - Messiah son of Joseph. Some rabbis believe he will suffer and serve like Joseph and eventually die in battle against the forces of darkness, to prepare the world for the final coming of the greater Messiah, son of David, who will usher in God's rule on earth. We know that Jesus is both *Moshiach ben Yosef* and *Moshiach ben David*, both the suffering servant and the King of Glory, and will indeed come again at the consummation of the Kingdom of God, as King of Kings and Lord of Lords. Hallelujah!

 Pray the Word

Praise God that the same Spirit of God that indwelt Joseph and Jesus, dwells in you, if you are a member of His Kingdom family.

Pray for a daily infilling of the Spirit of God to give you wisdom and power in your daily circumstances, for His glory and the blessing of many around you. **Pray** *'that the God of our Lord Jesus Christ, the Father of glory, may give you a spirit of wisdom and of revelation in the knowledge of him [God]'* (Ephesians 1:17).

Pray for the Lord to raise up righteous rulers in the nations, especially Israel and Egypt, who will be open to the Spirit of God guiding them into the ways of peace and prosperity. *Then Pharaoh said to Joseph, "Since God has shown you all this, there is none so discerning and wise as you are"'* (v39).

Pray for nations where there is famine and hunger today and ask the Lord in His mercy to provide food. *'Blessed is he whose help is the God of Jacob…who gives food to the hungry'* (Psalm 146:5, 7). **Pray** that governments and those who administer famine relief will have wisdom and integrity so that aid reaches those who really need it, and ask God to place His people in positions of responsibility where they can make a difference.

'And Joseph said to his brothers, "Please come near to me." So they came near. Then he said: "I am Joseph your brother, whom you sold into Egypt. But now, do not therefore be grieved or angry with yourselves because you sold me here; for God sent me before you to preserve life"' (Genesis 45:4, 5).

 Passage for study and prayer: Genesis 44:18 – 45:16

The way to this amazing moment when Joseph made himself known to his brothers had been a strange and tortuous one. From the time when they had first come into Egypt seeking food, Joseph had known who they were, but they did not recognize him. How could they? He was to all appearances a foreigner, an Egyptian of fearsome power and authority – not at all like their despised little brother! On his part, he wanted to find out if they had repented and changed since they treated him so cruelly. So he put them through a long and elaborate test, with suffering along with inexplicable blessings (see chapters 42-44). His brothers found it all mystifying and terrifying, as did their father Jacob too, back in the land of Canaan. For Joseph himself it was both joyful and painful, often reducing him to tears.

The final stage of the test was to manoevre his beloved younger brother Benjamin, who was the son of his own mother Rachel, into his own previous situation of unjust slavery, to see how they would react. Judah, the very one who had suggested selling Joseph to the Ishmaelites, dared to come near to him (44:18) to plead to be Benjamin's substitute, and it was this sacrificial response of genuine love, for his father's sake, that pushed Joseph beyond control. He burst into tears and sent everyone else out of the room, while he spoke in their mother tongue, 'I am Joseph'. His brothers were stunned by this revelation and at first were unable to believe it, but he finally convinced them that in spite of what it looked like, he really was their brother!

Moreover, he assured them repeatedly that it was God, not them, who had sent him into Egypt, for purposes of salvation and deliverance. They were to come and be near him, to be provided for during the lean years ahead. The family would be reconciled, and Jacob reunited with all his sons. And of course we know that they were being set up by God for the Exodus from Egypt, the event four hundred years later which would define their identity as a people and be pivotal in our understanding of the Kingdom of God.

 Pray the Word

Praise God that He always has a purpose even in the most difficult-to-understand circumstances! **Pray** that you may always come to Jesus in times of fear or insecurity or pain and trust Him to work things out for your good and His glory. *'And we know that all things work together for good to those who love God, to those who are the called according to His purpose'* (Romans 8:28).

Pray fervently for the Jewish people today to see beneath the Gentile disguise that Jesus wears and recognize Him as their brother and their Messiah, sent by God to bring them salvation. *'And now your eyes see, and the eyes of my brother Benjamin see, that it is my mouth that speaks to you'* (v12).

Pray too for the church in the nations to be like Pharoah and the Egyptians, and recognize their responsibility to help care for the brethren of Jesus. May there be a great outpouring of His love through Christians to Jewish people wherever they are found. *'When the report was heard in Pharaoh's house, "Joseph's brothers have come," it pleased Pharaoh and his servants'* (v16).

53

'Now there arose a new king over Egypt, who did not know Joseph. And he said to his people, "Behold, the people of Israel are too many and too mighty for us. Come, let us deal shrewdly with them, lest they multiply'" (Exodus 1:8-10).

 Passage for study and prayer: Exodus 1:1–2:10

In the *Torah*, the second book of Moses is known as *Shemot*, 'Names'. This passage starts with the names of the sons of Israel who came into Egypt, and it ends with the name of Moses. He was given that name by Pharaoh's daughter because 'Moses' means 'pull out', and she had pulled him out of the water (2:10). Names are very important in the Bible, as they express character as well as calling and purpose, and surely it's no coincidence that the meaning of Moses' name sums up the central theme of the book.

As the curtain rises on this momentous drama, we meet the main characters. The descendants – *ben,* literally 'sons' – of Israel (v9), have multiplied greatly over the generations, to become the twelve tribes of Israel. They are no longer favoured relatives of a foreign saviour, but cruelly oppressed slaves. Centre stage is Pharaoh, the king who did not study history, and only sees the growing Hebrew population as a threat to his power and security, and an opportunity for economic gain. Moses is waiting in the wings. Other characters are the Hebrew midwives, Shiphrah and Puah, whose names literally mean 'bright' and 'shining'. They introduce us to the most important One of all, God Himself, because it was their respect for Him that kept them from obeying Pharaoh's command to kill all the boy babies they delivered.

In Exodus, we see God not only as the Creator of the Universe, but as the Lord of history – His Story – who orders the affairs of men for His own purposes. He is in control of nations, and no earthly ruler can stand against His plans. Pharaoh tried everything he could think of to limit the Hebrew population, but nothing worked against God's covenant promise to bless and multiply them! The more the slaves were oppressed, the more they grew in numbers, and even the midwives because of their obedience became founders of families (v21). It is the ultimate irony that as a result of his desperate attempt at a 'final solution', Pharaoh ended up with a Hebrew boy growing up in his palace as an adopted member of his own family, who would one day lead the very escape from Egypt that the king feared and tried so hard to prevent (v10).

 Pray the Word

Praise God that He is indeed Lord of history, overruling all circumstances to bring about His plans for the nations. **Ask** Him for wisdom and insight as you follow the daily news, to help you pray for His Kingdom agenda. *'Of Issachar, men who had understanding of the times, to know what Israel ought to do'* (1 Chronicles 12:32).

Proclaim His sovereignty over Israel, Egypt and the other nations of the Middle East, and pray that the complex and painful situation there will result in the growth of God's Kingdom. **Pray** for local believers to be yielded to God and led by His Spirit so that, like Moses' mother, they can be blessed in fulfilling His purposes. *"'Take this child away and nurse him for me, and I will give you your wages.'"* (v2:9). Also **pray** special protection for Egyptian Christians, where Pharaoh's strategy to assimilate Hebrew women by killing a generation of Hebrew men has an echo in modern efforts to kidnap Christian girls and force them to marry Muslims.

Pray too for God to intervene to save the lives of unborn babies at risk through abortion. *'But the midwives feared God and did not do as the king of Egypt commanded them, but let the male children live'* (v17). Attempting to wipe out the coming generation has long been a strategy of the kingdom of darkness. **Pray** for countries where economic hardship encourages abortion, such as India, and for China where many girl babies are killed because of government policy allowing only one child per family.

THE BURNING BUSH

'Now Moses ... led the flock to the back of the desert, and came to Horeb, the mountain of God. And the Angel of the LORD appeared to him in a flame of fire from the midst of a bush' (Exodus 3:1, 2 NKJV).

 Passage for study and prayer: Exodus 3:1-15

Moses, out on a routine day at work, was not expecting to experience a world-shaking, life-changing event – just as other shepherds, at Jesus' birth, didn't either. Yet in both cases, God came down, after 400 years of silence, and revealed Himself in the midst of a very everyday situation. The bush was exactly like thousands of others in the lonely Arabian desert: scrubby, thorny, ordinary – except for one thing. It was aflame with the divine presence, the *shekinah* of God, and so it burned without being burned up.

Moses approached to take a closer look, and was amazed to hear his name. God spoke to him from the bush, about His nature and identity, His name and His purpose for His people. He first revealed His holiness – a burning, shining awe-inspiring otherness that kept Moses at a distance, shoeless with hidden face. He then declared Himself as the God of Abraham, Isaac and Jacob, Moses' forefathers. Notice that as He went on to explain why He had come down, the account uses His covenant name, the LORD (v7), only revealed to Moses later in verses 13-15. It was because of His covenant-keeping faithfulness to His people, as much as His compassion (v7), His power (v8) and His justice (v9), that He would deliver them from cruel bondage in Egypt into the blessing of the good land He had promised to their forefathers.

And He would do it through Moses, His chosen instrument (v10). Moses immediately questioned his fitness for the task, no doubt remembering his failure and flight 40 years earlier, but the Lord's answer was simple: "I will certainly be with you." His continuing presence would be the source both of Moses' authority and ability.

Notice that the sign He gives Moses is in the future –the "proof of the pudding" would be in the eating of it! One day he would be back at this very mountain, but with a different flock; one that would join him in serving God. We can miss the point in modern translations, but the King James Version makes the Hebrew clear: *'When **thou** (Moses) hast brought forth the people out of Egypt, **ye** (all of you) shall serve God upon this mountain'* (v12). Moses in the meantime had to obey in faith. The God who went on to say that His Name is 'I AM', the eternal ever-present One who was, is and forever will be (vv13-15), would be with him every step of the way.

 Pray the Word

Praise God that He has come down and revealed Himself to you through His Word and His Son the Messiah, and that He calls you by name! Respond to His voice as Moses did: *'And he said, "Here I am"'* (v4). Pray for grace and faith to fulfil His Kingdom commission for you.

Pray for a greater revelation of God's holiness, His nature and character, throughout the church, so that worship may be sincere and appropriate and result in power-filled obedience to His word. *'Then He said, "Do not draw near this place. Take your sandals off your feet, for the place where you stand is holy ground"'* (v5).

Pray for your own and all church leaders to hear His voice clearly and to be empowered by His Spirit, His indwelling Presence, so that they may lead His people into fuller service to God. *'So He said, "I will certainly be with you …When you have brought the people out of Egypt, you shall serve God on this mountain"'* (v12).

Pray for the Lord to call and equip more leaders for the ministry of powerful deliverance from the Kingdom of darkness, in your own and other nations: *'Come now, therefore, and I will send you to Pharaoh that you may bring My people, the children of Israel, out of Egypt'* (v10).

'I will take you as my people, and I will be your God. Then you shall know that I am the LORD your God, who brings you out from under the burdens of the Egyptians. I will bring you into the land which I swore to give to Abraham, to Isaac, and to Jacob; and I will give it to you for a heritage: I am the LORD' (Exodus 6:7, 8).

 Passage for study and prayer: Exodus 6:1-13, 7:1-6

Having called Moses to be the leader of His people, God uses him to call them all into a special relationship with Himself. He will take them to be His own *am,* His people in the sense of a tribe or congregated unit (v7- different from the more common term, *ben* or children of Israel), and will reveal Himself to them in a new way. This two-fold process involves both a bringing out, and a bringing in. They will be brought out from Egypt, delivered from their burdens and bondage and 'redeemed', that is, 'bought back' out of slavery, into relationship with Himself (v6). But the process will not be complete until they are brought in to possess their heritage in the land God gave to their fathers (v8).

All this was a bit too much for the slaves to cope with! Although they had kept their Hebrew identity, they had lost hope in the God of their fathers, and His covenant promises to give them their own land. However, God had not forgotten them. He heard their groaning and remembered His covenant, and He was preparing to do something spectacular to show them Who He really is (v5).

In vv2-6, God stresses His covenant name, YHWH, 'I Am Who I Am', (also meaning 'I Will Be Whom I Will Be') as the next stage in His revelation to His people. Though Abraham, Isaac and Jacob didn't know Him by this name, their descendants living in the midst of another religious culture needed to understand that their God was utterly different from the gods worshipped by the Egyptians. His covenant name underlined His nature – the eternal, ever-present, ever-faithful One who cannot ever go back on the

58

promises He made to their fathers. They were about to experience His mighty power and become His own special people even though their ongoing suffering and their broken spirit kept them from listening to Moses and believing God's Word (v9). In spite of their inability to respond, the LORD would bring them out from slavery and into the land of His promise, because He is faithful.

 Pray the Word

Praise the LORD that His eternal covenant-keeping nature is to keep His promises - always! **Pray** about difficult situations that you or others in your family or church may be facing and ask Him to reveal His mighty power through them. *'And I have also heard the groaning of the people of Israel, and I have remembered my covenant'* (v5).

Give thanks that we are not only delivered out of the Kingdom of darkness, but also delivered into the Kingdom of light. **Pray** for those suffering from a broken or anguished spirit that keeps them from receiving God's Word and experiencing the blessings of His Kingdom. *'...they did not listen to Moses, because of their broken spirit and harsh slavery'* (v9).

Pray for those who are enslaved in our world today (a simple internet search will provide information). **Beseech** the Lord to release His compassion and power on behalf of the millions of men, women and children who are trafficked, exploited or forced to work without basic rights. **Pray** for those who reach out to them and seek justice for them. *'The LORD works righteousness and justice for all who are oppressed'* (Psalm 103:6).

Pray that they may come to know the LORD who loves and delivers them. *'Then you shall know that I am the LORD your God who brings you out from under the burdens of the Egyptians'* (v7).

59

'Then the LORD said to Moses, "Go in to Pharaoh and say to him, 'Thus says the LORD, Let my people go, that they may serve me'" (Exodus 8:1).

 Passage for study and prayer: Exodus 8:1-23

The account of the plagues in Exodus is a bit like a tug of war. The children of Israel are the rope, pulled between Pharaoh and his magicians on one side and the LORD, their covenant-keeping God, with His spokesmen Moses and Aaron, on the other. It is a clash of kingdoms, a contest to show who is the strongest, who has the most authority, the most right to rule. The conflict had a spiritual dimension, as the Egyptians would have recognized; each plague clearly shows the Creator's power over one of Egypt's many gods, several of them associated with the Nile, the life-blood of the nation. And as they progress, God's power increases whilst that of the Egyptian magicians decreases and then ceases – compare verse 7 with verse 18. By the fourth plague, of flies, God demonstrates control of both space (v22) and time (v23), and His people in Goshen are already experiencing some freedom and protection from the effects of God's intensifying judgments.

However, this passage also teaches that freedom is never an end in itself. We all serve someone, even if it is the god of self. We know the refrain of the old spiritual song – 'Let my people go' – but we forget the end of the biblical sentence (vv1, 22). The purpose of the freedom was not only to deliver the slaves from their suffering, but to release them into service to another – the LORD Himself, to whom they truly belonged. The word 'serve', *abad,* is also used in Exodus 1:13: 'So they ruthlessly made the people of Israel *work* as slaves'. It basically means to work, but it can also mean to worship, to submit to one far greater than oneself. In Egypt, the children of Israel were forced to submit to their taskmasters, but after their deliverance they would be free to serve their God in the context of a loving covenant relationship. True, the slaves would be exchanging one kind of service for another, but there is a world of difference between forced submission to a cruel and oppressive system and free submission to a loving God who only wants the best for His people.

 Pray the Word

Give thanks that you are delivered from the kingdom of darkness; no longer a slave to sin, but a bondservant of the living, loving God and His Messiah! *'Giving thanks to the Father, who… has delivered us from the domain of darkness and transferred us to the kingdom of his beloved Son'* (Colossians 1:12, 13). **Pray** for grace to worship Him in all your daily work: *'I appeal to you therefore, brothers, by the mercies of God, to present your bodies as a living sacrifice, holy and acceptable to God, which is your spiritual worship'* (Romans 12:1).

Praise God that He is still more powerful than all false idols and demonic forces of wickedness. **Pray** for those in bondage to Satan's kingdom to see the power of God at work in His people, and come to know Him. *'But on that day I will set apart the land of Goshen, where my people dwell… that you may know that I am the LORD in the midst of the earth'* (v22). **Pray** especially for those involved in the occult to recognise His power to set them free: *'Then the magicians said to Pharaoh, "This is the finger of God."'* (v19).

Pray protection and power for those who are called to challenge the powers of darkness through intercession and deliverance ministry. **Pray** for discernment and obedience to the voice of the Holy Spirit in every situation. *'Be it as you say, so that you may know that there is no one like the LORD our God.'* (v10). **Pray** too for the church to fulfil its mandate as a spiritual witness to God's plan through the Messiah: *'so that through the church the manifold wisdom of God might now be made known to the rulers and authorities in the heavenly places'* (Ephesians 3:10).

PHARAOH'S HARDENED HEART

'But the LORD hardened the heart of Pharaoh, and he did not listen to them, as the LORD had spoken to Moses' (Exodus 9:12).

 Passage for study and prayer: Exodus 9:1-35

That's not fair! This is often the response from many in our humanistic, twenty-first century world, to any suggestion that God's sovereignty might overrule man's free will. Why should Pharaoh be punished because God had decided to make him stubborn and unrepentant, for his own purposes? Well, actually, he isn't. The truth is, of course, that he is being punished for things he has already done, and being confirmed in his own choice to ignore the LORD. (Paul graphically describes the same process in Romans 1: 18-32.)

Pharaoh was already guilty when God's judgements began. The Egyptians had kept Israel in painful bondage for generations, and even the suggestion that he should release them caused him to react with vindictive cruelty (ch5:2, 6-9). As the LORD's judgments progressed, it's interesting to note that from the start onwards, Pharaoh continually hardened his own heart (7:13, 22; 8:15, 19, 32). The first five plagues gave him ample chance to repent, before we read of God's hardening (literally 'strengthening', v12).

The trouble is that one sin leads to another. Anger and resentment were added to greed and pride, especially after the Lord had begun to protect the Israelites in the midst of the plagues (vv4, 7). After the terrible plague of hail, Pharaoh showed remorse and acknowledged his sin (v27), but it wasn't real repentance – once the hail stopped, he and his officials hardened their hearts again (vv34, 35). He was not willing to accept God's prior claim on His people, to acknowledge that God had the right to rule over them and receive their service. This is the background to the subsequent complete destruction of Pharaoh and those who stood with him.

Think about it - without judgment, there can never be real deliverance. As the LORD pointed out to Pharaoh in v15, He could just wipe out the lot of them with pestilence and that would be the end of that – freedom for His people! But His purpose is to do so much more (v16). He wants to reveal His name (that means the whole of who He is), not only to Israel, but to Egypt and all the nations of the earth, down through the ages. He also longs to show His mercy to all who will receive it. Look at verses 19-21 – He gave instructions about avoiding the plague of hail and all Pharaoh's people who believed and heeded His word were safe in the midst of the storm.

 Pray the Word

Search your own heart for any signs of hardness against the purposes of God for your life. **Ask** Him to keep you soft towards His word, that you may reflect His character. *'Sow for yourselves righteousness, reap in mercy; break up your fallow ground, for it is time to seek the LORD, till He comes and rains righteousness on you'* (Hosea 10:12 NKJV).

Pray for the LORD to raise up leaders in Israel, Egypt and the nations of the Middle East whom He can use to fulfil the purposes of His Kingdom. *'But for this purpose I have raised you up, to show you my power, so that my name may be proclaimed in all the earth'* (**v**16). **Pray** too for deliverance for those who are suffering in nations ruled by cruel dictators, and for the growth of the church in those nations.

National sin against the principles of God's word still results in God's judgments today. **Pray** that God's judgment on your own nation will be mixed with a mighty outpouring of His grace so that many will fear His Word and enter His Kingdom. *'Then whoever feared the word of the LORD among the servants of Pharaoh hurried his slaves and his livestock into the houses'* (v20).

PASSOVER: THE FEAST OF FREEDOM

'For the LORD will pass through to strike the Egyptians, and when he sees the blood on the lintel and on the two doorposts, the LORD will pass over the door and will not allow the destroyer to enter your houses to strike you'
(Exodus 12:23).

 Passage for study and prayer: Exodus 12:1-39

This pivotal biblical event lays the foundation of redemption, the purchase of a people for the purposes of God. It teaches us that death, the inevitable result of sin, is also the price of freedom. The Passover was life in the midst of death, deliverance in the midst of destruction and judgment, the first Feast of Freedom alongside the final, most devastating, plague which struck directly at Pharaoh himself. The Hebrew slaves were at last redeemed, but the price was high, and paid in blood. Every single Egyptian family lost a first-born son, from Pharaoh down to the lowliest prisoner, as the destroyer passed through each village and town and entered each home. No one escaped.

Except those who had a substitute, provided by God's grace for those who would respond in faith. Israelite families who obeyed the Lord's instructions through Moses brought a yearling lamb, a perfect specimen, into their home four days before. They made it a pet, a member of the family (vv3-6). On the eve of Passover, they slaughtered it on the doorstep and with a brush of hyssop, painted its blood on the lintel of the door and on each doorpost. (Picture it: blood above, below and to the right and left – does it remind you of anything?) This blood was a sign that a substitute had already died in the place of the firstborn son, and it meant that the Lord passed over their doorway as he executed His judgments on Egypt and its gods (vv12, 13). The lamb then formed a feast for the families, with bitter herbs and bread that did not need time to rise, to give them strength for what lay ahead. They ate it dressed for the journey, ready to flee as soon as the signal came (v11).

And this was to be a Feast forever (vv. 14, 17, 24). Every single year until the end of time, Israel must re-enact this Passover drama with their children, and observe the Feast of Unleavened Bread for seven days. God was saying that the price paid for His marvellous redemption, the lamb and the blood, must never be forgotten. A time would come when God's own first-born Son would be graciously given as that spotless lamb, slaughtered at the very moment of the Passover sacrifice so that his blood could cover all those who by faith received him as their substitute, and thus escape His judgment on sin to enter into the freedom of life in His Kingdom.

 Pray the Word

Praise the Lord that you have been 'passed over' for judgment because of the death of your Passover Lamb! **Pray** that you may live daily in the reality of freedom from your old slave nature. *'Clean out the old leaven, that you may be a new lump, since you truly are unleavened. For indeed Christ, our Passover, has been sacrificed'* (1 Corinthians 5:7).

Pray that the church worldwide may rediscover the full significance of Passover as the Hebraic background to Easter, and be greatly strengthened by the deeper understanding of God's Word that this brings. *"It is the sacrifice of the LORD's Passover..." And the people bowed their heads and worshipped'* (v27).

The Jewish *haggadah* or Passover liturgy, compiled in the first centuries of the Christian era, contains many elements which point to the death and resurrection of Jesus. **Pray** that as Jewish people celebrate it year by year, their Messiah will reveal Himself to them by His Spirit as their Passover Lamb. *'Now it was the Preparation Day of the Passover, and about the sixth hour. And he said to the Jews, "Behold your King!"'* (John 19:14)

'You will bring them in and plant them on your own mountain, the place, O LORD, which you have made for your abode, the sanctuary, O Lord, which your hands have established. The LORD will reign forever and ever' (Exodus 15:17, 18).

 Passage for study and prayer: Exodus 15:1-18

Did you know that according to the Jewish sages, this marvellous song of Moses contains Scripture's first explicit reference to the Kingdom of God? God's Kingdom is simply His Kingship, His sovereign rule or reigning, not just in a general sense over all creation, but specifically over a nation or people, who in turn relate to Him as their King. The Hebrew verb in verse 18 is not a simple future tense. It is more accurately translated "reigns", but with the sense of continuing on into the future - the Kingdom is already a present reality, but also will be everlasting, going on forever and ever. It is also a very active concept. God's rule is shown by His actions, in this case His miraculous deliverance of the children of Israel from the armies of Pharaoh, through the waters of the Red Sea. (Think of this when you next read what Jesus taught about the Kingdom of God, and how He demonstrated it!)

These verses are also the first recorded song of praise to the King in the Bible. They express so many of His attributes: His power over His creation, His wrath in judgment of those who withstand His purposes and commit evil, His compassion and mercy upon His people whom He has redeemed. He is the only God, far above all other gods, the all-powerful One who has purchased His people out of their slavery. But this redemption was not simply because He had compassion on their suffering, but to reveal to them, and to the nations round about, His power and glory.

He also brought them out to bring them in to the land He designated for His own special dwelling place. The LORD desires to live in the midst of His people. We see in these final verses, the interrelationship between the King, His people and a specific geographical location that continues right throughout Scripture. He established His sanctuary, His sacred set apart space where He chose to centre the revelation of His Kingdom, on a particular mountain in a particular location in our world. That place is still peculiarly His, and always will be, as we find when we read the end of the story! The Song of Moses (Revelation 15:3) and the city of Jerusalem (Revelation 21) will endure into eternity and the final consummation of God's Kingdom.

 Pray the Word

Praise the LORD that He is the King, the Creator of the Universe, the one in control of all nations and kingdoms, who loves His people and wishes to redeem them and bring them under His rule. This King is your God! *The LORD is my strength and song, and He has become my salvation; He is my God, and I will praise Him; my father's God, and I will exalt Him'* (v2).

Proclaim the power of the Lord to overthrow all the forces that stand against His purposes for His Kingdom, in the lives of His redeemed (including you!) and in communities and nations. **Pray** that He will act to show His power through His people: *'Your right hand, O LORD, has become glorious in power; Your right hand, O LORD, has dashed the enemy in pieces. And in the greatness of Your excellence You have overthrown them that rose against You; You sent forth Your wrath; it consumed them like stubble'* (vv6, 7).

Pray for God's mercy to be shown afresh to the people of Israel, who are still loved by Him and play an important role in His Kingdom purposes for the nations. May many more be drawn from exile and planted in the Land, and there enter into His presence and receive revelation of the Messiah. *'You in Your mercy have led forth the people whom You have redeemed; You have guided them in Your strength to Your holy habitation'* (v13).

'Then the LORD said to Moses, "Behold, I am about to rain bread from heaven for you, and the people shall go out and gather a day's portion every day, that I may test them, whether they will walk in my law or not"' (Exodus 16:4).

 Passage for study and prayer: Exodus 16:1-31

Just as a baby has to learn to walk as it grows, so the infant nation of Israel had to learn to walk in God's *torah,* His teachings or ways. As they journeyed through the wilderness, every part of their daily lives was used to teach them the principles of living as His people, receiving His blessings as they did things His way. Six weeks after leaving Egypt, when food supplies had run out, it was time for a lesson in the LORD's character, and how to trust and obey Him.

The hungry Israelites had forgotten in the pressing need of the moment, both the horrors of their slavery and the mighty power of their God. They whined and wailed like tired toddlers denied sweets in the supermarket – blaming their leaders, but really grumbling against the LORD. Moses and Aaron had to point them to Him, who alone could meet their need (vv8-10). The huge flocks of quail that dropped among their tents that night, and the mysterious white flakes covering the ground next morning, were proof that He was YHWH their God (v12), and committed to caring for His own. The quail satisfied their immediate hunger, but the manna was so much more – it became an ongoing blessing and lesson in daily bread. The people could choose to boil or bake it, but it had to be gathered early each day, and gathered God's way. However much or little they had strength to scrape up, it always measured just enough. Everyone was provided for, with no room for greed, or laziness. They couldn't store any 'just in case' – those who did not trust for tomorrow saw their hard work turn to stench and maggots. The only exception was on the sixth day, when a weekly miracle of double provision that did not deteriorate enabled them to keep the Sabbath as a day of rest.

This is the first time the Sabbath is specifically mentioned in Scripture. It is God's gracious gift of a day off from daily work – something slaves in Egypt knew nothing about! Provision of the manna established the weekly cycle of work and rest for God's people, patterned after the order of creation. Keeping the Sabbath holy, set apart for the LORD, would not only provide the blessing of rest but remind them weekly that their daily bread was the gracious gift of their Creator, and give them the chance to submit joyfully to His Word and will for their lives.

 Pray the Word

Praise God He can be trusted lovingly to provide our needs, both for sustenance and rest! **Give thanks** for ways He has provided for you, and **pray** that you may carry out your daily tasks diligently and with joy, according to God's Kingdom principles in His word. *'Whatever you do, work heartily, as for the Lord and not for men; knowing that from the Lord you will receive the inheritance as your reward'* (Colossians 3:23, 24).

Pray for those experiencing hunger or want, especially believers in the nations who are persecuted for their faith, or who live in other circumstances of poverty. May the LORD reveal Himself to them as their provider: *'At twilight you shall eat meat, and in the morning you shall be filled with bread. Then you shall know that I am the LORD your God'* (v12). **Pray** for those whom He uses to bless the poor and needy.

Pray that God's people may learn that ignoring God's Kingdom principles brings barrenness: *'On the seventh day some of the people went out to gather, but they found none'* (v27), whilst walking in obedience to His word brings blessing and maturity, and joy to God's heart. *'Oh, that my people would listen to me, that Israel would walk in my ways!'* (Psalm 81:13). **Pray** too that in our stressful 21st century lives, Christians will obey God's instructions to set aside one day in seven to rest and draw closer to Him.

'Moses built an altar and called the name of it, The LORD Is My Banner, saying, "A hand upon the throne of the LORD! The LORD will have war with Amalek from generation to generation"' (Exodus 17:15, 16).

 Passage for study and prayer: Exodus 17:8-16

At the Red Sea, the LORD had finally and forever delivered Israel from Pharaoh's armies. The Israelites hadn't had to lift a finger, so it was probably a shock to realize that as free men, they had to fight to keep what God had given them! When marauding Amalekite tribesmen fell upon the vulnerable rear of their caravan to steal, kill and destroy (see Deuteronomy 25:17-18), Moses understood that the battle to move forward in God's purposes was spiritual as well as physical. He appointed Joshua to lead the troops, whilst he went up to high ground with the rod of God in his hand.

That rod was the symbol of YHVH and all that His name stood for. It became a *nes* in Hebrew, a standard or ensign, a banner declaring that the LORD Himself was in charge, sovereign over the battle. It reminded the warriors who they were fighting for, and why – and no doubt intimidated the enemy too! Above all, it was a concrete expression of Moses' trust in God's word, His character, His power. As long as he was able to hold out the truth of the LORD's promises and purposes above the battle, the ground was held, but if the *nes* was lowered, the enemy prevailed. The strength or skill of the soldiers was not the key, but Moses' strength to hold up the standard. He couldn't do it alone, and Aaron and Hur had to help his hands remain 'steady' until the battle was finally won. The word *emunah* means firm, steadfast, and faithful. Moses' faithful, faith-filled holding to God's authority and power ensured complete victory (v13).

The Amalekites, descendants of Esau, were not totally destroyed, but they would be (v14). This attack on the Israelites sealed their final fate, because they were actually attacking the LORD Himself. Israel's destiny was to be a people amongst whom God would dwell and rule, His throne in their midst for all to see. Amalek had dared to touch the throne of the King, and that meant the King declared war on them until their final destruction (v16). And Israel was never to forget, in all future battles, the only source of their victory: *YHVH-nissi* – 'the LORD is my banner' (v15).

 Pray the Word

Praise God that He is 'YHVH-nissi', your battle standard. Declare His truth and promises over every attack aimed at hindering God's purposes for your life, or that of your family, church or community. *'Whenever Moses held up his hand, Israel prevailed'* (v11). **Pray** for strength to press through in prevailing prayer until victory comes.

Pray for those who are weak and vulnerable, as new believers or because of ill-health, difficult circumstances or battle fatigue in pioneer situations: *'he attacked you on the way when you were faint and weary, and cut off your tail, those who were lagging behind you, and he did not fear God'* (Deuteronomy 25: 18). **Declare** God's grace and power over them to *'be strong in the Lord and in the strength of his might'* (Ephesians 6:10).

Pray for many intercessors to be raised up to pray for spiritual leaders, at home and in the nations, to strengthen them to remain faithful and focussed in their calling to lead God's people into His purposes: *'Aaron and Hur held up his hands, one on one side, and the other on the other side. So his hands were steady until the going down of the sun'* (v12).

Pray that persistent and prevailing intercession will enforce the Lord's victory and authority in every situation where His enemies seek to stop the progress of His Kingdom.

'Jethro said, "Blessed be the LORD, who has delivered you ... out of the hand of Pharaoh and ... the people from under the hand of the Egyptians. Now I know that the LORD is greater than all gods' (Exodus 18:10, 11).

 Passage for study and prayer: Exodus 18:1-27

God always intended His people to be a witness to those without knowledge of Him. After the Amalekite attack, Moses must have been encouraged when his father-in-law Jethro arrived with Zipporah and their two sons. Jethro the Midianite priest, like the Amalekites, was a distant cousin of the Israelites (via Abraham and Keturah) – yet his reaction to God's people was very different. We don't know what gods the Midianites worshipped, but Jethro was obviously a devout man, and the account of the LORD's mighty works made a huge impact on him.

As he sat with Moses in his tent, we can picture his eager questions about what had happened since he had last seen his son-in-law, when he was about to head back to Egypt after his amazing call from God in this very place. His response to Moses' testimony of the difficulties and blessings experienced thus far shows he was both godly and astute. Firstly, he rejoiced at all the LORD had done for Israel (v9). Sadly, people often respond with jealous anger rather than rejoicing, even today! Secondly, he praised and blessed the LORD Himself, acknowledging His mighty power (v10). And thirdly, he realised who the LORD was – greater than all other gods, not just in His power, but in His love and righteousness (v11). He had a revelation of His character, and this led to faith and worship, and a symbolic joining of himself to the people of God through a fellowship meal (v12).

However, that wasn't all. Jethro went beyond his faith in Israel's God, to love and bless God's people too. He used his wisdom and expertise to help Moses organise His time and workload more effectively, to keep him from wearing himself out in ministry (vv13-

23). These principles of delegation, oversight and training those with potential and character to do the work of God, are still the foundation of effective leadership in God's Kingdom today. Jethro's two-fold response is a perfect example for us to follow. Israel's calling to be a light to the nations, and bring them the knowledge of the true God, has never changed. Even today, God reveals His Word as truth through His dealings with the Jewish nation, and seeks to use Gentiles who believe in Him as an instrument of guidance and blessing.

 Pray the Word

Rejoice that you have come to know Israel's God and enjoy the benefits of adoption into His family, and pray that you may give of your gifts and talents to bless His ancient covenant people as He leads. *'Comfort, comfort my people, says your God'* (Isaiah 40:1). Pray that others will do the same.

Pray for God to graciously reveal Himself and His Son Jesus to multitudes of men and women in the nations who worship other gods in ignorance, yet with great devotion. **Pray** for anointing on those who witness to them with their testimony of all the LORD has done for them according to His Word. *'Then Moses told … how the LORD had delivered them'* (v 8).

Pray for leaders who are suffering through overwork and the demands of ministry. Ask God to provide wise counsel and show them how to spread the load: *'What you are doing is not good. You and the people with you will certainly wear yourselves out, for the thing is too heavy for you. You are not able to do it alone. Now obey my voice'* (vv 17-19).

Pray for biblical patterns of leadership to be established in your church and in God's Kingdom worldwide: *'Moreover, look for able men from all the people, men who fear God, who are trustworthy and hate a bribe, and place such men over the people as chiefs of thousands, of hundreds, of fifties, and of tens'* (v21).

'Now therefore, if you will indeed obey My voice and keep My covenant, then you shall be a special treasure to Me above all people; for all the earth is Mine. And you shall be to Me a kingdom of priests and a holy nation' (Exodus 19:5,6a).

 Passage for study and prayer: Exodus 19:1- 23

Almost seven weeks after Passover, the Israelites came to Mount Sinai, just as God had promised Moses. Here He would reveal Himself again, this time to all His people, to take them into a new, adult relationship with Himself. The mighty miracles of their deliverance were not merely to redeem them from their slavery and bondage and return them to the land of their forefathers. No, the LORD had something greater in mind – nothing less than a wedding!

Relationship is at the heart of all God's acts. The Hebrew word translated 'special treasure', is *segullah*. It means something very precious, especially chosen and set aside for someone's exclusive use or adornment. (Check out Psalm 135:4, Ecclesiastes 2:8 and Malachi 3:17 for other occurrences of the word). The Lord is saying that he has chosen this people above all others, as a man chooses a beloved bride. He has brought them out of Egypt 'on eagles' wings' – literally supporting them like a parent eagle - to bring them, not to a place, but to a person, Himself. They are the 'house of Jacob' and the 'children of Israel', and because of His promises to their patriarchs, He will enter into a new dimension of covenant relationship with them. Unlike the eternal and unconditional covenant with Abraham, however, this Mosaic covenant is conditional and will involve new kingdom responsibilities on Israel's part.

Notice the word 'if' (v5). If they obey God's voice and keep the covenant, Israel will be a 'kingdom of priests', consecrated entirely for loving service to their King. They will be holy; 'set apart' in the midst of the nations, bearing God's name, reflecting His character and helping fulfil His purposes in His earth. Now, having solemnly accepted God's proposal with a pledge to listen and obey (v8) they were to prepare themselves over the next three days to meet their bridegroom and take their vows to Him. Just as a bride stands on the threshold of a new, adult life with new joys and responsibilities, so does this fledgling nation at Mount Sinai.

 Pray the Word

Rejoice that Jesus has redeemed you to become part of His bride, and join you to God's holy Kingdom of priests! Pray for a deeper relationship with Him, leading to a greater witness to those around you. *'But you are a chosen race, a royal priesthood, a holy nation, a people for his own possession, that you may proclaim the excellencies of him who called you out of darkness into his marvellous light'* (1 Peter 2:9).

Pray for unity in the Body of the Messiah, based on a united commitment to obey the truth of His Word. *'And all the people answered together and said, "All that the LORD has spoken we will do"'* (v8). **Pray** too for Jewish people to understand that they are still God's special treasure, and reaffirm their allegiance to the LORD and His Word to them.

Pray for the church in its world-wide witness in every nation, to so proclaim the truth of the Kingdom, that multitudes may give their allegiance to the King and so extend His reign throughout the earth. *'by your blood you ransomed people for God from every tribe and language and people and nation, and you have made them a kingdom and priests to our God, and they shall reign on the earth'* (Revelation 5:9, 10).

'And God spoke all these words, saying, "I am the LORD your God, who brought you out of the land of Egypt, out of the house of slavery. You shall have no other gods before me"' (Exodus 20:1-3).

 Passage for study and prayer: Exodus 20:1-21

At Sinai, the mountain of revelation, the LORD spoke to the people of Israel directly for the first time. It was exactly 50 days after the Passover redemption – the first Pentecost! Whilst the context conveys the awesome, overwhelming power of the experience for the Israelites, verses 1-17 distil the essence of what He said. The 'ten words' are a summary of the covenant between God and His people, expanded and expounded in detail in the rest of the Torah. (Jesus summarised them even further, see Matthew 22:37-40). Interestingly, the commandments are all spoken to 'you' in the singular. They applied to every single individual personally, and each one had to take personal responsibility for obeying them.

Note that keeping the law was not the basis of Israel's salvation, for that had already happened (v2). It was **because** they were redeemed, that they now had laws to help them live God's way and serve Him amongst the nations. The commandments (*mitzvot,* see verse 6,) provided the moral base of their culture as God's people, very different from the Egyptian and Canaanite cultures that reflected life without the knowledge of God. That is why Israel's relationship with the LORD was paramount (v3), and any form of idolatry or service to another god was absolutely forbidden (vv4-6). They were not to take the LORD's name in vain – that is, speak or act in any way that would shame His name and nature (v7). They were to honour His order in creation, both through observing the Sabbath and honouring their parents through whom they had received life (vv8-12). Relationships with one another were to be based on truth and on respect for each other's life, marriage, and possessions (vv13-17), reflecting the character of God Himself and protecting the cohesion of their society.

These laws are not negative, but express the mutual commitment of the King and His people. God is jealous for His beloved bride and wants her for Himself alone (v5). Breaking the boundaries will bring iniquity, *avon,* a twisting from God's ways that will continue to corrupt succeeding generations – but keeping them will strengthen the bond with God that is founded on *chesed* (v6). This word, often translated 'lovingkindness' or 'mercy', is always used in the context of mutual commitment. It is better expressed as 'covenant loyalty'. The LORD's steadfast, faithful covenant love and loyalty is assured to those who reciprocate by hearing and obeying His Word.

 Pray the Word

Thank God for His moral blueprint for Kingdom living. As you reflect on this passage, ask the Holy Spirit to show you if you are breaking His boundaries in any way. **Pray** to be set free from any form of idolatry and claim His power to sanctify His Name as you live your life for His glory. *'If you love me, you will keep my commandments'* (John 14:15).

Pray for the church to reflect God's moral standards through obedience to His Word, rather than the values of the surrounding culture. *'Therefore whoever relaxes one of the least of these commandments and teaches others to do the same will be called least in the kingdom of heaven, but whoever does them and teaches them will be called great in the kingdom of heaven'* (Matthew 5:19). **Pray** for exposure and rejection of the lie that the 'law' of God's commandments is no longer relevant, and for clear teaching of Kingdom values in the church.

Pray too for your community and nation, for a turning to biblical standards that will bring new life and strength to families, institutions and society as a whole. **Declare** these commandments as God's truth and **proclaim** that where there is obedience to God's ways, there will be His blessing: *'Righteousness exalts a nation, but sin is a reproach to any people'* (Proverbs 14:34).

MARRIAGE CONTRACT

'Behold, I send an angel before you to guard you on the way and to bring you to the place that I have prepared. Pay careful attention to him and obey his voice; do not rebel against him... for my name is in him' (Exodus 23:20, 21).

 Passage for study and prayer: Exodus 23:1-33

Today, Jewish couples still draw up a *ketubah*, a traditional pre-nuptial contract outlining their personal goals and mutual obligations for their marriage. God's *ketubah* with His people is the Book of the Covenant, found in Exodus chapters 21-23. Most of it fleshes out the Ten Words summary with examples and principles to guide Israel in applying them in daily life. For example, in 23:1-19 look for references to false witness, justice and respect for the lives and property of others, Sabbath rest, idolatry and the right way to worship God – cooking a kid in its mother's milk was a Canaanite fertility ritual! Right at the end, in verses 20-33, the LORD outlines His part of the contract. It centres on the promise of His *malak,* angel or messenger, to guide and guard His people into the possession of their dowry, their full inheritance as His bride. Who is this angel? Well, whether he manifests at different times as the visible pre-incarnate Messiah or the unseen Holy Spirit, (or even Israel's guardian angel Michael), we know the LORD's name is in him (v21), He speaks with God's voice and is to be carefully listened to and obeyed (v22). As Isaiah says, 'the angel of His presence' (63:9) assures Israel of the LORD's presence, power and victory to overcome every enemy and obstacle – as long as they keep their side of the bargain!

As a loving husband, God is preparing them a home in the Promised Land, and promises all the resources they need for a full and happy life together with Him. He will provide food and water, health, fruitfulness and prosperity (vv25-26) in return for their loving service. Verse 25 is one of only two verses in Exodus that speak of healing, and it clearly links physical health with living God's way (cf 15:26, also Deuteronomy 7:15). The sound hygiene and health benefits of many Torah laws are borne out by modern medicine, whilst, conversely, idolatrous practices carried many risks to health. Where God rules, health and healing usually follow, as Jesus demonstrated so powerfully in His earthly ministry.

Notice that overcoming is a gradual process. In God's providence, Israel must possess the Land step by step, so that they can consolidate each gain as they grow in strength (vv29, 30). They must also claim the ground for Him alone (v24). There is no room for compromise with their enemies, whose gods will trap them into sin (vv32-33). The *ketubah* is always conditional, and continued victory depends on continued faithfulness. Sadly, we know they failed. Though fully redeemed from Egypt, they never fully obeyed and thus never enjoyed their full inheritance as the wife of the King (v30).

 Pray the Word

Praise God for the riches of our inheritance in the Messiah, and the promise of His help in overcoming the enemy of your soul! **Pray** for grace to overcome in the battleground of your mind against all forces of wickedness: *'you shall not bow down to their gods nor serve them, nor do as they do, but you shall utterly overthrow them'* (v24). *We destroy arguments and every lofty opinion raised against the knowledge of God, and take every thought captive to obey Christ'* (2 Corinthians 10:5).

Praise too for His promise of health and prosperity for those who walk in His ways, and pray that Christians will demonstrate its reality to those around them. *'You shall serve the LORD your God, and he will bless your bread and your water, and I will take sickness away from among you.'* (Exodus 23:25).

Pray all the promises of verses 27-30 for those who are advancing God's Kingdom in pioneer situations, whether at home or in the nations. *'For the weapons of our warfare are not of the flesh but have divine power to destroy strongholds'* (2 Corinthians 10:4). **Pray** for wisdom and divine strategy to possess the land God's way.

79

'Then he took the Book of the Covenant and read in the hearing of the people. And they said, "All that the LORD has said we will do, and be obedient." And Moses took the blood, sprinkled it on the people, and said, "This is the blood of the covenant which the LORD has made with you according to all these words"' (Exodus 24:7, 8 NKJV).

 Passage for study and prayer: Exodus 24:1-18

A royal wedding! This chapter resonates with the solemnity and grandeur of a state occasion, and includes all the elements of an ancient covenant ceremony between a king and a subject people. First, terms and procedure are agreed. Only certain ones may approach the King, and only Moses may come close (vv1-2). Moses explained God's words one more time to make sure the people understood, and they responded together: *na'aseh v'nishma*, literally 'we will do and we will hear' (v3, see also 19:8). This was not just intellectual assent – to hear or listen in Hebrew always implies understanding and action.

Then, the deal is solemnly sealed in blood. The Hebrew word for 'making' a covenant is *karat,* meaning to 'cut', because biblical covenants usually involve the shedding of blood. Blood symbolizes life and also death should the covenant be broken, and it stresses the serious and binding nature of the agreement, and unites the parties as 'one blood' in their commitment to each other. Moses built an altar, along with twelve pillars, one for each tribe. Oxen were sacrificed and half the blood was sprinkled on the altar, representing God. After a formal reading of the Book of the Covenant, Israel pledged a third time to hear and obey (v7), and the remaining blood was sprinkled on the pillars that stood for the people. Just as the blood of the lamb had provided the covering for each family to be redeemed from the angel of death, so now the covering of God's protection and blessing was over the nation as a whole – as long as they remained loyal to the King.

The agreement, the vows, the signing – then the party! Sharing a covenant meal cements and celebrates the new relationship. Moses, Aaron with his sons Nadab and Abihu, and seventy tribal elders were invited up to the high table to banquet with the King. This high honour, to see something of the majestic, awesome God of Israel, and eat and drink before Him without being struck down (vv9-11), was only possible because of the blood of the covenant. Finally, there is the 'sign of the covenant', a lasting witness to promises made (see e.g. Genesis 9:12, 17:11). God called Moses to 'Come up' again to receive the stone tablets, along with further instruction (v12). Leaving Aaron and Hur in charge, this time he went right to the summit into the fire of God's glory. Israel saw it all, but only from a long way off (vv14-18).

 Pray the Word

Praise God that though Israel failed to keep this covenant, He cut a new one with them in which you can share, and draw close to Him. *'This cup that is poured out for you is the new covenant in my blood'* (Luke 22:20). *'But now in Christ Jesus you who once were far off have been brought near by the blood of Christ'* (Ephesians 2:13).

Pray for Jewish people everywhere to receive the blessing of the new covenant: *'I will make a new covenant with the house of Israel … not like the covenant that I made with their fathers … that they broke, though I was their husband, declares the LORD … I will put my law within them, and I will write it on their hearts … no longer shall each one teach his brother, saying, 'Know the LORD,' for they shall all know me …For I will forgive their iniquity'* (Jeremiah 31:31-34).

Pray for those who teach God's Word to spend quality time in His presence, to receive His guidance and anointing: *'Come up to Me on the mountain and be there; and I will give you … the law and commandments which I have written, that you may teach them'* (v12, NKJV).

'And let them make me a sanctuary, that I may dwell in their midst. Exactly as I show you concerning the pattern of the tabernacle, and of all its furniture, so you shall make it' (Exodus 25:8, 9).

 Passage for study and prayer: Exodus 25:1-22

During Moses' forty days on the mountain, the LORD revealed His detailed plan for His future daily relationship with Israel. He was not going to stay distant from them, up in the heavenlies – quite the contrary. He was coming down to live amongst them! They were to build a holy sanctuary, a *mikdash,* from the root *kadash,* meaning to make clean, or purify. This would be the Tabernacle, the *Mishkan,* from the root *shakan,* to dwell - a home for God's living presence at the heart of their nation. It was to be built exactly to God's pattern (v9), of the finest materials – the King's royal tent in the midst of the camp!

The blueprint started with the most important item, the ark. This chest, made of wood overlaid with gold to symbolize the human and divine parties involved, was to hold the testimony or witness (*edut*) of the covenant (vv16, 21). It had poles to carry it without touching it, for it was holy. The ark also served as the base for the mercy seat, the *kaporet.* This biblical word comes from *kaphar,* meaning 'to cover' or 'atone', and as well as covering the ark it was also where Israel's sin was covered every year, on *Yom Kippur,* the Day of Covering or Atonement (see Leviticus 16:15, 16). The mercy seat was made of pure gold (can you think why?), with two winged cherubim, one rising and arching over it from each end (vv19, 20). These angelic beings that barred the way to God's presence in Genesis 3:24 would now symbolically see the covering for Israel's sin. The sacred space between was where the divine presence would dwell (the *shekinah,* also from *shakan*), and light the darkness of the Most Holy Place with the divine glory. From here, on the firm base of the covenant, the holy God would continue to meet and communicate with His people.

Notice however, that not just anyone could approach the Ark of the Covenant. Later chapters show that the tabernacle mirrored God's threefold order of Exodus 24:2. The people could approach the outer court to bring their sacrifices, and the priests could enter the Holy Place to minister in daily worship, but only Moses, the chosen mediator, could freely enter the Holy of Holies into the shining presence of the LORD (v22). The High Priest would also have that honour, but only once a year. Although the King dwelt amongst His people, He was still the King.

 Pray the Word

Praise God that Jesus came down to be a living fulfilment of the *Mishkan*, to tabernacle amongst us to reveal the Father's glory, and open the way for all into His presence through his own blood. *'And the Word became flesh and dwelt among us, and we have seen his glory, glory as of the only Son from the Father, full of grace and truth'* (John 1:14). **Pray** for a greater revelation of His glory and holiness.

Pray for Christians everywhere to understand more fully the relationship of God's covenant to His ongoing presence, power and revelation to His people: *'And you shall put the mercy seat on the top of the ark, and in the ark you shall put the testimony that I shall give you'* (v21). **Pray** they may use His Word, the testimony of His covenant love, as a powerful tool of witness to unbelievers.

Pray also that believers may realise the privilege of intimacy with a holy God, and so worship Him in spirit and truth, that they may enter the Holy of Holies to hear His Word to them by His Holy Spirit: *'There I will meet with you, and from above the mercy seat, from between the two cherubim that are on the ark of the testimony, I will speak with you about all that I will give you in commandment for the people of Israel'* (v22). **Pray** this especially for those in leadership.

'Then bring near to you Aaron... and his sons with him, from among the people of Israel, to serve me as priests... And you shall make holy garments for Aaron your brother, for glory and for beauty' (Exodus 28:1, 2).

 Passage for study and prayer: Exodus 28:1-43

Mark Twain once famously said that "clothes make the man". Well, certainly the priestly garments made Aaron the High Priest. A whole chapter is devoted to his ceremonial clothing, with detailed instructions about every article – even his underwear! Without the holy garments, he was simply Aaron the Israelite. Only his robes, in all their symbolic meaning, gave him the right to stand before a holy God on behalf of the people, and before Israel to represent, and speak for, God.

The garments were to impart something of God's glory and beauty, made of the finest materials by those with spiritual anointing for the task (vv2-8). Their colours, of gold, blue, purple and scarlet as well as pure white linen, speak of deity, of heaven, of royalty, of sacrifice, and of purity. Of the seven items, four set the High Priest apart from other priests: the blue robe, fringed with woollen pomegranates and gold bells, the colourful apron-like ephod, the breastplate and the turban. As he went about his duties of service and worship, Aaron would bear the names of the 12 tribes engraved on two stones on his shoulders, the place of strength. Their individual names were also carried over his heart, each engraved on a different jewel on the breastplate, as a reminder of the LORD's love for them (v29).

The breastplate also had a special function of judgment, forming a pouch holding the Urim and Thummim, meaning 'flames' and 'perfections' – articles that revealed God's will and decisions in specific situations (v30). A pure gold plate was suspended from the turban across Aaron's forehead, symbolically covering his mind and thoughts and inscribed with the words: 'Holy to the LORD'. God thus saw him as holy, and that is why he could present the people's sacrifices to cover their sin (vv36-38).

And so the high priestly robes defined Aaron's role as an intercessor and mediator. Like God, he was to carry the weight of the nation on his shoulders and heart, interceding for them as he offered their sacrifices and sought counsel in decision-making. His acceptance represented the peoples' acceptance by the LORD and his holiness, like theirs, came from submitting to God's way of worship and sacrifice. However, beneath the robes and despite a special anointing for the task (v41), he remained a sinful man. Later, One would come who did not need outward robes to be our Great High Priest, and through His offering, all who believed in Him could receive the Holy Spirit, and real power to live a holy life.

 Pray the Word

Praise Jesus for being your Great High Priest, Intercessor and Mediator! **Pray** for greater insight into His priestly role and how it affects you: *'Consequently, he is able to save to the uttermost those who draw near to God through him, since he always lives to make intercession for them. For [we] have such a high priest, holy, innocent, unstained, separated from sinners, and exalted above the heavens'* (Hebrews 7:25, 26, see also Hebrews 4:14-16).

Pray for pastors and leaders to have God's heart for those they serve and pray faithfully for them: *'So Aaron shall bear the names of the sons of Israel … on his heart, when he goes into the Holy Place, to bring them to regular remembrance before the LORD'* (v29). **Pray** for guidance in judging difficult pastoral situations: *'And in the breastpiece of judgment you shall put the Urim and the Thummim…Thus Aaron shall bear the judgment of the people of Israel on his heart before the LORD regularly'* (v30).

Pray that leaders may live genuinely holy lives, daily submitting to God and resisting the enemy, in the power of the Holy Spirit. **Pray** especially for victory in their thought life: *'You shall make a plate of pure gold and engrave on it… Holy to the LORD… It shall be on Aaron's forehead'* (vv36, 38).

'And the LORD said to Moses, "Go down, for your people, whom you brought up out of the land of Egypt, have corrupted themselves"' (Exodus 32:7).

 Passage for study and prayer: Exodus 32:1-35

How had the Israelites corrupted, or ruined, themselves? In less than 40 days they had turned aside from God's way, so carefully explained by Moses and which they had three times solemnly vowed to keep. They ganged up on Aaron to demand he make them a god that they could see to lead them forward. Their sin was to worship an idol and call it the LORD; reducing their holy, all-knowing, all-powerful, 'totally other than' Creator and Redeemer to an object made with human hands that fitted into their human understanding (vv4, 5). Thus their sacrifices and feasting inevitably degenerated, like all pagan worship, into irreverent, abandoned revelry that destroyed their calling to be a redemptive community amongst the nations (vv6, 25). Tragically the very gifts God had intended for their blessing became tools of their ruin – the golden calf replaced the mercy seat.

How did this happen, and so quickly, to a people who had experienced so much of God's power and love? Well, lack of leadership undoubtedly played a part. Moses was absent, and Hur isn't mentioned – some Jewish commentators think this may mean he was killed for resisting the mob. Aaron was clearly intimidated and allowed fear of man to overcome fear of God. His failure to protect the people from themselves made his own sin the greater, though he refused to admit it (vv21-24). However, the main answer from God's perspective is that Israel is a stiff-necked people (v 9). The image is that of the conquered refusing to place his neck under the heel of the conqueror. In other words, they refused to submit to God and His word because they were rebellious by nature. Idolatry is simply the result of the determination to "do it my way", and God despaired of them ever being able to keep the covenant. He would destroy them utterly because they were beyond redemption, and replace them with Moses' descendants (v10).

What happened next? Moses, unlike Aaron, acted as a true priest. He interceded for the people, beseeching God to spare them on the basis of His character and reputation (vv11-14). Then he went down to deal with Israel. In his fury that mirrored the LORD's, he smashed the stone tablets, just as Israel had smashed God's covenant. He destroyed the golden idol and made the people drink its dust. He confronted Aaron and made sure that the ringleaders of the rebellion were executed. Then he offered his own life as atonement for them. This was not accepted – God made it clear that each man was responsible for his own sin, and would face the consequences – yet in His grace He did not utterly destroy them (vv30-35).

 Pray the Word

Pray that God will speak to you from this passage about any idols in your life. **Thank** Him for Jesus, the 'one like Moses' who was able to give His life as atonement for your sins, and what's more, give you a new heart to free you from your rebellious nature! *'Moses said, "The Lord God will raise up for you a prophet like me from your brothers. You shall listen to him…"'* (Acts 3:22).

Pray for the many in our post-modern age who claim to be Christian but worship a god made in their own image, rejecting the parts of God's word that they don't like and refusing to submit to His Kingship. *'They have turned aside quickly out of the way that I commanded them'* (v8). **Pray** for God's mercy to bring revelation, repentance, and restoration by the power of the Holy Spirit.

Pray for a fresh and powerful revelation in today's church of the seriousness of sin, and how it destroys our witness to a needy world. *'Aaron had let them break loose, to the derision of their enemies'* (v25). **Pray** especially for leaders in their great responsibilities, to fear God more than they fear man.

'Go up to a land flowing with milk and honey; but I will not go up among you, lest I consume you on the way, for you are a stiff-necked people' (Exodus 33:3).

 Passage for study and prayer: Exodus 33:1-23

God deeply desires intimacy with man – that's why He created him – but His burning holiness cannot tolerate sin. He would allow Israel to leave Sinai and inherit the land because of His promises to their patriarchs, but He could not go with them personally. His presence, like fire, would destroy them. They had demanded a god in their midst, which was what the LORD intended all along – but they forfeited it through idolatry. No wonder when they heard this disastrous word, all Israel mourned (v4). They took off their ornaments (plunder from the Egyptians and associated with pagan worship as well as their own recent sin), and humbled themselves in genuine repentance and obedience (vv5-6). But with the covenant broken, they were separated from their Husband, their King.

However, Moses took a tent and pitched it outside the camp boundaries. An ordinary tent, not at all like the glorious kingly tabernacle in their midst that God had planned, it was 'far off' (v7) – yet still much closer than the summit of Sinai! Everyone could see the LORD come down as a pillar of cloud to meet with Moses at the doorway, and could worship from afar (v10). Joshua spent every possible moment in the 'tent of meeting' (v11). He had not broken the covenant, yet by God's grace even those who had taken part in Israel's sin could make the effort to come apart and seek His will and ways if they really wanted to do so (v7).

Yet Moses knew what God's original purpose was. He longed for His presence to be manifested in glory and majesty right amongst His people. So he prayed, something like this: "Who are you going to send with me when we leave here? Please, let it be You. If you won't come, I don't want the milk and honey! And remember that my people are your people too, and what's more, Your reputation is at stake!" (vv12-16).

The LORD loved this prayer. He knew Moses, understood his heart, and would do all he asked (v17). But when Moses asked for more, to see His glory (v18), He could only reveal His 'back' – His goodness, mercy, and the 'covenant saving faithfulness' expressed in His name YHWH – the part of His nature that assured Moses that His sovereign grace still ruled. He would have to cover and shield him from the 'face' of His burning justice and holiness. The root meaning of *kavod,* 'glory', is 'heaviness' – and even Moses could not bear the full weight of seeing all that God is (vv19-23).

 Pray the Word

Praise God that through Jesus you may freely enter His presence, for yourself and also on behalf of others. **Pray** Moses' prayer to know Him better, and live to please Him: *'...please show me now your ways, that I may know you in order to find favour in your sight'* (v13).

Pray for God's people to be delivered from a form of religion without the living presence and power of God. *'Please let me see your glory'* (v18). May they turn from all that keeps Him at a distance in their worship and service. *'Indeed, I count everything as loss because of the surpassing worth of knowing Christ Jesus my Lord'* (Philippians 3:8).

Pray for repentance and restoration for believers who have fallen into sin. *'When the people heard this disastrous word, they mourned...'* (v4). **Pray** for revelation of God's mercy but also of the seriousness of sinful behaviour, and a willingness to change and obey His Word: *'Therefore the people of Israel stripped themselves of their ornaments'* (v6).

Pray for offenders in prison to own and repent of their crimes against individuals and society. **Pray** for chaplains and ministries to be empowered by the Holy Spirit to help prisoners seek God's forgiveness and new life in His Kingdom. *'And everyone who sought the LORD would go out to the tent of meeting, which was outside the camp'* (v7).

'Be ready... and come up in the morning to Mount Sinai, and present yourself there to me on the top of the mountain... Three times in the year shall all your males appear before the LORD God, the God of Israel' (Exodus 34:2, 23).

 Passage for study and prayer: Exodus 34:1-35

God summons Moses to 'come up' Mount Sinai once again for another appointment with Him (v2). In a fresh and further revelation of His Name and character, the LORD declares He is full of mercy, compassion and grace, slow to anger and overflowing with *chesed v'emet*, covenant love and truth (or faithfulness, reliability). For this reason, He will forgive rebellious Israel, even though His justice does not allow sin's consequences to be entirely removed (vv 5-8). He will rewrite the memorial tablets and renew the covenant, and bring Israel into their land with mighty signs and wonders – but they must remain faithful to Him alone, for He is a jealous God (vv9-17).

He also re-establishes a cycle of special appointments with Himself, through which His people will maintain their exclusive relationship with Him as they celebrate who He is and what He has done for them. As well as the weekly Sabbath when they will rest and remember Him, no matter how busy they are (v21), they are to 'go up' into His presence three times each year to worship Him with their offerings (vv20, 26), trusting Him to protect and provide for them (v24). The three biblical Feasts are both agricultural and commemorative. The spring Feast of Unleavened Bread (*Pesach*) is a memorial of Israel's deliverance from Egypt. The Feast of Weeks (*Shavuot*), fifty days later (hence Pentecost), offers the first grain of the harvest but also remembers the giving of the *Torah* and the covenant at Sinai. In the autumn, the harvest Feast of Ingathering or Tabernacles (*Succot*), celebrates God's dwelling with His people. Every year Israel celebrates the three Rs – Redemption, Revelation and Rejoicing in His presence!

These annual appointments to 'go up' to the LORD are profoundly important in God's Kingdom. Not only have they kept Israel a distinct people throughout history, focused on Jerusalem where the tribes 'went up' to meet with God (Psalm 122), they also have a wider prophetic fulfilment. Jesus died and rose again at *Pesach*, and the Holy Spirit was poured out on His disciples at *Shavuot*. The autumn holy days ending with *Succot* speak of Messiah's future return and reign over the nations. Notice too that the effect of keeping God's appointments is deeper fellowship with Him (v34), effective intercession (v9), and a powerful witness to others (v30). After the times he spent in the LORD'S presence, Moses literally reflected His glory!

 Pray the Word

Meditate on these wonderful verses and praise the LORD afresh for all that He is! *'The LORD... a God merciful and gracious, slow to anger, and abounding in steadfast love and faithfulness, keeping steadfast love... forgiving iniquity and transgression and sin, but who will by no means clear the guilty'* (vv6, 7). **Pray** for grace to keep regular appointments with Him, so that His glory and character will be reflected through you to others: *'Moses did not know that the skin of his face shone because he had been talking with God'* (v29).

Pray likewise for your Christian family and friends to receive a deeper revelation of God's character, leading to worship and greater submission to Him: *'And Moses quickly bowed his head toward the earth and worshipped'* (v8). May His life and love be strongly reflected through their lives.

Pray that the church worldwide will rediscover the prophetic significance of the biblical Feasts, and celebrate them as a witness in the nations: *'Then everyone who survives of all the nations that have come against Jerusalem shall go up year after year to worship the King, the LORD of hosts, and to keep the Feast of Booths'* (Zechariah 14:16). **Pray** too that the LORD will reveal His Word more fully through the Holy Spirit to His people Israel, as they celebrate the Feasts each year.

'Moses assembled all the congregation of the people of Israel and said to them, "These are the things that the LORD has commanded you to do"' (Exodus 35:1).

 Passage for study and prayer: Exodus 35:1-36:1

After the covenant was renewed, Moses called together the congregation – *edah* – of the sons of Israel. This wonderful word is first used in Exodus 12:3, as God is about to redeem Israel by blood to be His covenant nation. It is from the root *ed*, which means witness, or testimony, and carries the idea of community. God's people, the *Adat Yisrael*, are to be a witnessing community, a testimony of God's grace and power in an unredeemed world. Just look at the things the LORD commanded them to do.

First, they are to be distinct from all other communities. That is why they are to keep the Sabbath holy to Him, on pain of death (v2). *Shabbat* is vitally important, not just to test Israel's obedience and give them needed rest, but as a witness to those around them. Second, they are to give to God from what He has given to them (v5). Men and women, young and old, from the leaders to the least, all have precious things to dedicate to the LORD, as they respond in their hearts and spirits to His love and grace. Every need is met as everyone generously offers what he has, on a strictly freewill basis – nothing forced here! Third, their offerings are to build a dwelling place for God's presence in their midst (v21). Every single thing they needed for the tabernacle had already been supplied (see Exodus 12:35-36), even though they were former slaves, wandering through the desert and living on manna! Fourth, they are to give not only materially, but of their God-given skills and abilities, to share in creating this wonderful home for their God (vv10, 25).

Notice that the LORD called Bezalel 'by name' and equipped him with all that was needed to carry out God's blueprint – skill, intelligence, knowledge, craftsmanship, creativity – by filling him with the Spirit of God (vv30-33). To these spiritual gifts for Bezalel, and for his assistant Oholiab, He added another vital one -

the inspiration and ability to teach (v34). The work of building God's dwelling place on earth was not only for a few specially gifted leaders. These gifts were also to equip others to share in that service, just as Paul wrote to the Ephesians (4:12). As each used their gifts for God's glory, members of the *Adat Yisrael* would work together under His inspiration to demonstrate something of His own glorious, creative nature. And just as they witnessed to His abiding presence with them when His glory filled the tabernacle (see Exodus 40:34), so the *Adat Yeshua,* the witnessing community of Jesus, is called to be filled with the presence and power of the Holy Spirit, testifying to the reality of His Kingdom in the midst of a needy world.

 Pray the Word

Thank the LORD that you are part of the *Adat Yeshua,* Jewish and Gentile believers in Jesus who are witnesses to God's Kingdom rule! **Pray** for a stirring up of the spiritual gifts God has given you and others to build up His *edah* in your community, for His glory: *'And they came, everyone whose heart stirred him, and everyone whose spirit moved him, and brought the LORD's contribution'* (v21).

Pray for willing hearts to give all that is needed for the work of God worldwide, whether it be financial resources, time, skills or energy, so that there is no lack in any part: *'All the men and women… whose heart moved them to bring anything for the work that the LORD had commanded by Moses to be done brought it as a freewill offering to the LORD'* (v29).

Pray for a great outpouring of the Holy Spirit to manifest God's glory through His witnessing community, as His people submit to His rule in holiness and obedience to His Word: *'Then the cloud covered the tent of meeting, and the glory of the LORD filled the tabernacle'* (40:34). **Pray** for God's Kingdom to come and His will to be done throughout the earth, as it is already purposed in heaven. (Matthew 6:10).

RECOMMENDED FOR FURTHER STUDY

A Taste of Torah – A Devotional Study through the Five Books of Moses
by Keren Hannah Pryor, Center for Judaic-Christian Studies
www.jcstudies.com Available in the UK from www.cfi.org.uk

Celebrate Jesus! – A Christian Perspective of the Biblical Feasts
by Joan Lipis, Novea Ministries
www.novea.org   www.CelebrateJesusTheBook.com

Where on earth is God today?
by Desi Maxwell, Evangelical Publishing Ltd
Xplorations: the ministry of Desi Maxwell www.xplorations.org

See relevant websites for information on how to order, as well as
for more useful study material available online.

The 40 day format of the **Praying God's Word** series lends itself to personal reflection and prayer – especially at Lent. The prayer ideas are also helpful for small group prayer with the Bible reading and reflection helping people pray with insight.

You can obtain more for use in your church or small group in 3 ways:

- Via your local Christian bookshop
- Via www.amazon.co.uk
- By ordering from *Praying God's Word*

Three resources are available at this time.

Praying for the Peace of Jerusalem
Helping you pray with biblical insight into God's agenda for Israel today.

Penny Valentine   Tahilla Press   ISBN 978-1-84291-187-2

Praying for Israel and the Arab Nations
Further biblical prayer for Israel and for God's salvation purposes for the surrounding nations.

Penny Valentine   Tahilla Press   ISBN 978-1-907228-07-0

Praying the Foundations of the Kingdom of God
Strengthening God's rule in your life and in the nations, through biblical prayer.

Penny Valentine Tahilla Press ISBN 978-1-907228-17-9

See over for order information

If ordering from *Praying God's Word* **please note the following:**

- Books are priced at £6 each
- Postage is an additional £1.60 (1-2 copies), plus £1 per book for 3 or more copies
- Make cheques payable to *P. Valentine*
- Write stating quantities and name(s) of books required to: P. G. W., The Old Chapel, Twitchen Clunbury, Craven Arms, Shropshire, SY7 7AN, UK

  Email: pennyprayer@gmail.com